THE
HIGH SCHOOL
SURVIVAL GUIDE

MAKING THE MOST OF THE
BEST TIME OF YOUR LIFE
(SO FAR)

ADAM PALMER

D0126538

NAVPRESS

NAVPRESS●®

NavPress is the publishing ministry of The Navigators, an international Christian organization and leader in personal spiritual development. NavPress is committed to helping people grow spiritually and enjoy lives of meaning and hope through personal and group resources that are biblically rooted, culturally relevant, and highly practical.

**For a free catalog go to www.NavPress.com
or call 1.800.366.7788 in the United States or 1.800.839.4769 in Canada.**

© 2008 by Adam Palmer

ISBN-13: 978-1-60006-129-5
ISBN-10: 1-60006-129-X

Cover design by www.studiogearbox.com
Creative Team: Rebekah Guzman, Heather Dunn, Cara Iverson, Darla Hightower, Arvid Wallen, Kathy Guist

Some of the anecdotal illustrations in this book are true to life and are included with the permission of the persons involved. All other illustrations are composites of real situations, and any resemblance to people living or dead is coincidental.

All Scripture quotations in this publication are taken from *THE MESSAGE* (MSG). Copyright © 1993, 1994, 1995, 1996, 2000, 2001, 2002, 2005. Used by permission of NavPress Publishing Group.

Library of Congress Cataloging-in-Publication Data

Palmer, Adam, 1975-
  The high school survival guide : making the most of the best time of
your life (so far) / Adam Palmer.
    p. cm.
  Includes bibliographical references.
  ISBN 978-1-60006-129-5
  1. Christian teenagers--Religious life. 2. Christian
teenagers--Conduct of life. I. Title.
  BV4531.3.P36 2008
  248.8'3--dc22

                                    2007042127

Printed in the United States of America

2 3 4 5 6 7 8 9 10 / 12 11 10 09 08

CONTENTS

ACKNOWLEDGMENTS

I would be remiss if I didn't take some time up front to acknowledge a few people, without whom this book would not have come to fruition. (And now I must apologize for opening this book for students with a sentence containing the words *remiss* and *fruition*. It won't happen again.)

First up: Nicci Hubert, who had the idea in the first place and convinced me to write it. I had no idea I would learn so much about God when I embarked on this little mission. Thanks for pushing me off the cliff.

Also, big thanks to my editor, Heather Dunn, for her most excellent input and chopping-up of my words. You brought more to the table than maybe you know.

Thanks to Rebekah Guzman, Kate Epperson, Kris Wallen, Arvid Wallen, and all the nameless, thankless people at NavPress for continuing to believe in me as an author and for all the effort you put into these projects. Many thanks to whoever designed this killer cover.

To Josh Kleehammer, whose priceless advice helped me shape the initial outline: a pound and a half of thanks.

Enormous thanks have to go to Troy Powell and Daniel McIntosh for setting up the student roundtable discussions for me. And to the students who participated—Alex, Andrew, Anna, Gabrielle, Grant, Haden, Hanna, Jaime, Jenava, Jennifer, Johnny, Josh, Kaitlin, Kat, Marley, Michael, Phil, and Tyler—you contributed far more than even I had anticipated. I had so much fun talking to you, and I learned a lot. Couldn't have done it without you.

Evan Taylor, I've never properly thanked you for the oh-so-smart-looking photo you took of me that has now graced three books. So consider this your proper thanks.

To my family: Thanks for your willingness to let me talk about you in this book. Hope I didn't embarrass you too much.

And lastly, to my wife, to whom I proposed on the day she *graduated* from high school: I can't believe we thought we knew what we were doing! Thanks for stumbling through this life by my side, for growing and maturing with me, and for your huge contribution toward making me the man I am today. And bigger thanks for being my best friend.

INTRODUCTION

To the high school student reading this book, I offer a single word: Congratulations. Congratulations on reaching this point in your life. Congratulations on making it through the trials of your early school years—the trials of finger-painting the alphabet in kindergarten; the trials of multiple-digit multiplication and long division; the trials of weekly spelling tests; the trials of memorizing presidents and state capitals; the trials of dissecting those disgusting frogs.

Well, maybe you haven't done that last one yet. Trust me, it ain't pretty.

You've outlasted some academic trials, but, as we all know, school is about so much more than academics. You also conquered the trials of being bullied on the playground at recess; the trials of skinning the cat on the monkey bars for the first time, in front of your friends, without showing fear; the trials of checking "yes" or "no" on a fateful note from a member of the opposite sex; the trials of choking down mystery food in the lunchroom.

Oh yeah: I guess there were some report cards and tests and stuff in there too.

Anyway, I offer my sincerest congratulations to you, high school student, whether you're staring with trepidation at your freshman schedule or looking forward with tired fondness to your senior year—or somewhere in between. You are at a remarkable time in your life, a crazy period when you leave childhood behind and take your first tentative steps into adulthood.

In short, to borrow a term from the military, you are in no-man's-land. A no-man's-land filled with all sorts of land mines and distractions: friends, family, temptation, peer pressure, a maturing body, cultural perceptions, popularity, self-image issues, running up your cell phone minutes, and countless others.

And in the middle of this craziness, you're expected to get an education.

I've been out of high school for a few years, and in those few years, a lot has changed for the typical American high school student. You're dealing with things that weren't even thought about, let alone mentioned, when I was in high school (and, honestly, it wasn't *that* long ago).

But parts of the high school experience remain ubiquitous (that's a five-dollar word that means essentially "everywhere at once") no matter when you experience them. The word *prom* most likely strikes the same amount of fear and anticipation into you as it did into me, especially if you're a skinny, Shakespeare-spouting, antisocial nerd like I was, with your nose in a book and your eyes on any and all semi-eligible members of the opposite sex.

Okay, maybe I'm exaggerating a little. (I've been accused of this occasionally.) I was actually just a regular ol' teenager like you—ready to assert myself in a more grown-up world, but still packed to the gills with insecurities about myself. Eager to navigate the challenges of high school, but still hesitant about meeting those challenges head-on. Confident on the outside, scared witless on the inside.

Perhaps you struggle with these same feelings. Perhaps, if you're honest with yourself, you need a little help tackling all the things life throws at you during those four years known as "high school."

You probably have a lot of questions about what's in store for you. We all do. You could be the most popular person on the football team, or the most book-smart valedictorian candidate, or the most rebellious troublemaker, or the sweetest blend-into-the-background student, or the most flexible member of the cheerleading squad, or the first-chair-in-concert-band kid, or the . . . well, you get the point.

No matter who you are, you are going to have big questions. Questions like:

* *What should I do when my parents get on my nerves?*
* *What is the opposite sex thinking?*
* *Does anyone like me? Anyone at all?*
* *How can I avoid making a total fool of myself?*
* *Does it really matter what movies I watch or what music I listen to?*
* *How can I do better in school?*
* *What are colleges looking for?*
* *Is there life after high school?*

And these questions only skim the surface of the high school experience. Then, even if you answer *them*, you still have the biggest question of them all: Where does God fit into all of this?

Look, I'm going to be honest with you up front (and

throughout the book) and tell you that I don't have all the answers—not the answers to the big questions of life anyway. But I've managed to figure out a thing or two about living, and God, and I want to share that wisdom with you to help you make the most of this very unique time of your life.

But there are going to be things you'll just have to figure out for yourself. All I can give you is information; it's up to you to apply it. It's up to you to figure out *how* that information relates to your academics, to your relationships, to your spirituality, to your self-image.

The good thing? You don't have to figure this stuff out on your own—God is on your side. You may be at a slightly scary, slightly anticipatory time of your life, but God isn't freaked out. Nothing that has ever happened has taken Him by surprise. Not to get into those thorny questions about why bad things happen to good people, or how God can allow genocide, or any of those types of things (that's a topic for a different book), but no one has ever thrown God a curveball. He's never thrown up His hands in frustration and said, "Well, I didn't expect *this*."

So this God, this God who isn't flustered by anything, this God who retains complete sovereignty over the world—this God is interested in *you*. And He was human once, so He understands the *very stage of life you're in*. Jesus was as much man as He was God, so He had to deal with this very same transition from childhood to adulthood.

He's been through it, and He can help you get through it too. All you have to do is ask.

I know *I've* asked, time and again. And these are a few of the things I've learned. . . .

CHAPTER 1

YOU

It's in Christ that we find out who we are and what we are living for. Long before we first heard of Christ and got our hopes up, he had his eye on us, had designs on us for glorious living, part of the overall purpose he is working out in everything and everyone. (Ephesians 1:11-12)

Love the Lord God with all your passion and prayer and intelligence and energy. (Mark 12:30)

Start with GOD—the first step in learning is bowing down to GOD; only fools thumb their noses at such wisdom and learning. (Proverbs 1:7)

WHO AM I? IS THERE MORE TO LIFE THAN JUST GETTING GOOD GRADES AND SCRATCH-AND-SNIFF STICKERS ON MY HOMEWORK?

"I don't know who I am yet, but I'm getting there."
— Tyler, 17

This is *the* question of our time. Our culture is on an insane search for purpose and meaning in life — entire books have been written about this very topic. Maybe you've read a few of them. Maybe you're on the same search and haven't figured it out yet.

There are specifics to that question that no one but God can answer. I can't sit on this side of the page and tell you what God wants you to do with your life in a specific sense. I can't tell you that God wants you to be a missionary or writer or nursery worker or Wall Street broker or barista at Starbucks or minister of the gospel through clowning or anything else you might choose to do with your life. That's for God to tell you.

But here's something I *can* tell you: Your purpose is to serve God.

I know! So easy to say, so difficult to do.

"There's no originality anymore. You can't be original. The only way to be original is to take the outside influences, these unoriginal things, and blend them to make something original." — Johnny, 17

Here's the deal: God just wants your heart. Plain and simple. He wants you to *want* to serve Him. You can act like you're serving all you want and do good things, but what truly pleases God are people who stick close to Him, who seek Him, who want with all their hearts to do whatever He tells them to do.

Look at Colossians 3:3-4. It says, "Your old life is dead. Your new life, which is your real life—even though invisible to spectators—is with Christ in God. He is your life. When Christ (your real life, remember) shows up again on this earth, you'll show up, too—the real you, the glorious you. Meanwhile, be content with obscurity, like Christ."

What does that mean for you? It means that the solution to the problem of life is easy: Just hang with Jesus. *That's* where your life is. There and nowhere else will you find the satisfaction that comes with knowing your purpose.

> "Knowing exactly who you are comes from the experiences you've had in life. The things you've participated in and the experiences you've had blend together to make you who you are. So that makes it hard at any point in your life to know exactly who you are, because there's always something new adding to it." — Jennifer, 17

And the Old Testament says the same thing: "Blessed is the man who trusts me, GOD, the woman who sticks with GOD. They're like trees replanted in Eden, putting down roots near the rivers—Never a worry through the hottest of summers, never dropping a leaf, Serene and calm through droughts, bearing fresh fruit every season."

That's Jeremiah 17:7-8, and it paints a marvelous word picture of what happens when you hang with God.

You get to be a tree, just hanging out by a river, never with a legitimate care about anything—doing nothing but producing a ton of fruit.

Pretty cool way to go through life, don't you think? Tossing out all the worries and headaches and drama, and just hanging with God. And the best part? You get to produce freshness for other people to snack on spiritually. When you're hanging with God, your life is going to have an impact on other people's lives. Give them something worthwhile.

It really is that simple. Don't sweat the details—God will give them to you when the time is right. Just pursue Him, and He'll take care of you.

"High school is so confusing because there are so many things coming at you, ways you want to act. When you're with friends, you pick up their mannerisms, so it makes it very difficult to find out who you are. But the way you really are is the way you are when you're by yourself." — Kat, 17

Not that it isn't work, mind you. It is. But it's work with a purpose, work that will bring about something good in the world, even if we can't see for sure what that good thing will be.

Paul liked to use a lot of metaphors in his writing, and this is one of his most potent: "You've all been to the stadium and seen the athletes race. Everyone runs; one wins. Run to win. All good athletes train hard. They do it for a gold medal that tarnishes and fades. You're after one that's gold eternally.

"I don't know about you, but I'm running hard for the finish line. I'm giving it everything I've got. No sloppy living for me! I'm staying alert and in top condition. I'm not going to get caught napping, telling everyone else all about it and then missing out myself"(1 Corinthians 9:26-27).

See, it's work. But it's worth it, because there's a reward at the end. And, from time to time, there are rewards along the way, but the big one comes at the end, after we've been "running hard for the finish line" and "giving it everything [we've] got."

That's when it all pays off and makes sense. Until then, we just need to keep running. Or, as in the earlier metaphor from Jeremiah, we just have to keep ourselves planted next to God. I know those two images seem like they don't go together (how can you be planted *and* running?), but they're just images to help us grasp the grander idea of God: Stick with Him, do what He says, and you'll be fine.

> "I like to challenge what I believe just so I can make my beliefs stronger. If people can't tell what I believe without me saying it, then I've done a really bad job of living my beliefs." — Tyler, 17

WHY AM I HERE?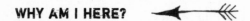

> "I've never asked myself why I'm here." — Kat, 17

You know who asked that question once? Esther. Queen Esther. A *long* time ago, back in Bible times. Like, before Jesus was around even.

Okay, so you know the Israelites, right? Well, in between the time of Moses and Jesus, the Israelites had their own country, but they messed around and turned their backs on God for too long. They wound up being overtaken by a country called Babylon, whose rulers made all the Israelites become second-class citizens.

Fast-forward a few years and suddenly the king of Babylon wants a new queen. He auditions a few prospects and settles on Esther, who happens to be an Israelite. A Jew.

Except the king doesn't know that.

I'm giving you the short version of the story here. There's another guy, Haman, who hated the Jews. Hated 'em. Wanted them all dead, and came up with a very sneaky plan to get rid of them. Basically, he had the king sign a law saying that on a specific day, it would be lawful for the Babylonians to kill as many Jews as they wanted, penalty-free. The Israelites couldn't do a thing about it.

Esther had a cousin named Mordecai, and he started pleading with her to do something about this situation. She didn't want her countrymen to die any more than he did, but she didn't know what she could do about it. The only thing that could stop the massacre was another decree from the king, but Esther wasn't really in a position to barge into the throne room and start making demands.

See, this king was a bit of a hothead. If he didn't send for you, you'd better not show up in front of him or he might do something crazy, like have you killed (I guess I overshot it with the word *bit* just then—the guy was a *definite* hothead).

So Esther found herself between a rock and a hard place. Did she expose her nationality to the king, risking his crazy wrath in the process, hoping that he liked her enough to prevent the slaughter of her people? Or did she sit tight and (hopefully) save her own skin? It was a test of her character. It was a chance for her to look inward and ask, "Why am I here?"

Uncle Mordecai had an answer for her, which we find in Esther 4:12-14: "Don't think that just because you live in the king's house you're the one Jew who will get out of this alive. If you persist in staying silent at a time like this, help and deliverance will arrive for the Jews from someplace else; but you and your family will be wiped out. Who knows? Maybe you were made queen for just such a time as this."

Mordy didn't really pull his punches, did he? He just lays it out, plain and simple: "Who are you? You're the queen, and your time for doing what God wants you to do is now."

"I'm sure no one can say what they're supposed to do in the world. Even if you shorten it down to high school, that's still a tough question to answer on your own. It helps if other people chip in and remind you of things you've done or things you could do." — Andrew, 16

This is an isolated example of the types of questions we ask ourselves all the time. Who are we? Why are we here? What's the point of all this? Specific answers, like the one Esther got, change as you go through life, but the general answers remain the same:

Who are you? You're God's child.

Why are you here? To please Him.

What's the point of all this? To trust God.

Faced with the decision, Esther summoned her courage and went before the king. She trusted God and didn't get struck by anything crazy. The king heard her request, sympathized with her, and changed up the game completely. He made a law that said the Jews could defend themselves on that same day. And when the day came, the Jews killed their enemies and were saved.

Wherever you are, God has a way to use you for His glory

and goodness. No matter the circumstance, no matter how you got there—whether it was through outside influences or your own screwups—God sees you and has something for you to do. You just have to trust Him.

> "Have I **ever** answered the question 'Why am I here?' No. God knows why I'm here. That's good enough for me. I'll figure it out someday."
> —Anna, 16

WHAT ABOUT MY OUTSIDES? DOES THAT STUFF MATTER?

If there's one thing that makes me sad about the world today, it's this: how much we judge people by the way they look on the outside. I'm in a coffee shop right now filled with the following people: a kinda nerdy-looking guy spreading note cards out on a table and tapping infrequently on his laptop; a heavily tattooed young woman pushing a baby stroller and talking loudly about how long she was in labor; an intellectual sleep researcher in hospital scrubs sipping tea; and a barista with a bushy beard and long hair who looks like either a crazy person or Jesus, depending on the light in the room.

I mention these people's outsides for one reason: When I first met them, I was wrong about each one of them as far as their amount of togetherness. The nerdy guy isn't really that nerdy—he just isn't stylish. The tattooed woman loves her baby as much as a mother can and lives a clean lifestyle. The sleep researcher is one of the most spiritually lost people I know. The barista is one of the most righteous people I know.

Still, there's a constant message from our culture that you have to look a certain way to be accepted, to the point where we have reality shows about clothes designers and hair stylists and, probably soon, manicurists and pedicurists and people who make fake eyelashes. Glamour is so popular that even anti-glamour punk-rock bands tour with hair stylists and makeup artists.

Whether you're into looking stylish or you go the opposite way and spend inordinate amounts of time proving you *don't* want to look stylish, there's a message from society: We're going to judge you on the way you look, so you'd better look good.

God's message runs countercultural to this notion, however, to the point of telling women in 1 Peter 3:3-4, "What matters is not your outer appearance — the styling of your hair, the jewelry you wear, the cut of your clothes — but your inner disposition." Granted this passage is written specifically to married women, but both guys and gals can take away the greater point: It doesn't matter to God how you look on the outside; it matters what you're doing with your insides.

Now, don't use this verse as a springboard to say, "Yay, I can wear whatever I want!" Because your outside *does* matter to the rest of us. First and foremost, you have to submit to your parents in this area — if they've forbidden the nose ring or tat, then don't go against their authority just because you want to. The Bible makes no real argument for or against that type of stuff, but it does tell you to honor your parents, so you pretty much have to. If you want to ink up when you're an adult, you can make that decision at that point.

And you have to consider your fellow believers. Girls, I'm going to let you in on a secret: Guys like looking at chicks.

No, really — it's true.

Guys, check this out: Girls are interested in guys. For real!

So, since you like to look at members of the opposite sex, and since you're generally wrestling some crazy hormones, you probably should steer clear of any temptations that might come your way. Temptations like staring at, and possibly fantasizing about, whoever wanders into your field of vision.

This is why it's important that you take care of *other peoples'* fields of vision. Dress appropriately and you have much less of a chance of accidentally enticing someone into sinful behavior.

"But that's *their* problem," you might say. "I don't have that problem, so I can do whatever I want."

A valid point, ordinarily. But let's take a gander at the Bible, where Paul is talking to the Corinthian church about that very thing. See, some of the Christians around there had a hard time eating food that had been sacrificed to idols. They felt that it was wrong; they couldn't see it as just a meal with a nonbeliever—to them, it was a sinful thing to do.

Other Christians had no problem with it and couldn't understand why anyone would, so they would go chomping on this food in front of the more sensitive folks and, essentially, create guilt in their minds to where they thought they had to eat that stuff too. Anyway, Paul sets everyone straight in 1 Corinthians 8:11-12: "Christ gave up his life for that person. Wouldn't you at least be willing to give up going to dinner for him—because, as you say, it doesn't really make any difference? But it does make a difference if you hurt your friend terribly, risking his eternal ruin! When you hurt your friend, you hurt Christ."

Of course, we aren't talking about food in the context of our discussion, but the principle remains the same: If you're going to do something that could hurt someone's walk with Christ, you're hurting that person, and you're hurting Jesus.

God's looking at your insides; the rest of us are looking at the outside. Make sure what *we* see reflects what *God* sees.

WHAT ARE MY WEAKNESSES, AND WHAT DO I DO ABOUT THEM?

I don't care how strong you are; I don't care how popular or hip or cool or outgoing you are—you have weaknesses. Everyone does.

But what do you do about them? (I mean, after you figure them out.) You still have to move forward with life, and part of that forward movement involves accepting and dealing with your weaknesses.

"We're taught, from the time that we're young, that everybody's different. And that's true—nobody thinks the same, nobody lives the same. And that's why there are a lot of problems. That becomes the excuse for everything. But when you get right down to it, we're all just human. Yeah, we don't think the same, but we're all just human. We're all people; not one of us is better than any of the others."—Kaitlin, 17

Maybe you're a little too wrapped up in your self-image. Maybe you're so lazy you sleep until three in the afternoon. Maybe you're doing destructive things to yourself, like self-inflicting wounds or developing an eating disorder. Maybe you're sleeping around. Maybe you aren't and have become a serial masturbator instead.

We all have weaknesses. We all have areas of our lives we have to give to God. We all have the deck stacked against us in one of the games of life.

I'm reminded of the famous story of David and Goliath, where this kid who seemingly had everything going against him entered a battle with a giant and found that he really had everything he needed.

You know the story, how David, the shepherd boy, killed Goliath with his sling and some stones, but I want to talk about what happened just before he went into battle. Saul, seeing David's youthful stature, outfitted the poor lad in some adult armor in the hopes of providing some "strength." David was having none of it though, telling Saul in 1 Samuel 17:39, "I can't even move with all this stuff on me. I'm not used to this." So he took it off.

And then he turned his perceived weakness—his shepherd-boy nature—into victory and kicked some major giant booty.

God has a way of flipping the script on the world. The Bible even comes right out and says it in 1 Corinthians 1:27-28: "Isn't it obvious that God deliberately chose men and women that the culture overlooks and exploits and abuses, chose these 'nobodies' to expose the hollow pretensions of the 'somebodies'?"

God is all about using our weaknesses to showcase His own strengths. See, your weaknesses become sin because the Devil uses them to trap you, to enslave you. But God wants to use those very same weaknesses to make *His* name known. God can take those weaknesses and not only help you through them but also help you use them to reach others for God.

IS THERE A DIFFERENCE BETWEEN WHO I AM AND WHAT I DO?

Yes, yes, yes. Most assuredly yes.

Have you read Romans 7:14-16? Paul talks about his seeming inability to live a Christlike life. It'll most likely be the same for you, because you're going to screw up this life. It's going to happen. Even if you were the most perfect person ever, the law of averages is against you and demands that you make a mistake or two at least once or twice in your life. And since you *aren't* the most perfect person ever, or even close, you're going to screw up *a lot.*

Does that make you a screwup? No way.

It just makes you human.

> "I definitely act differently around different people. Usually it's either to please them or to piss them off. Can I say that?" — Kat, 17

→ Now, you *are* responsible for your actions, especially if you know better. Consider this passage from Romans 2:12-13: "If you sin without knowing what you're doing, God takes that into account. But if you sin knowing full well what you're doing, that's a different story entirely. Merely hearing God's law is a waste of your time if you don't do what he commands. Doing, not hearing, is what makes the difference with God."

> "Humankind is very two-faced. The way you act does depend on who you're around. Around one group of friends, I can be very open and definitely be myself and be crazy, then with other friends I'm more quiet, or I act a certain way or dress a certain way around them. I don't do it consciously, but I notice it after the fact that I did that in order to fit in." — Jennifer, 17

You may have experienced the grace of Christ, but that doesn't mean you have license to go around doing whatever you want and then asking for forgiveness. By contrast, you're called to a higher standard: "Friends, this world is not your home, so don't make yourselves cozy in it. Don't indulge your ego at the expense of your soul. Live an exemplary life among the natives so that your actions will refute their prejudices. Then they'll be won over to God's side and be there to join in the celebration when he arrives" (1 Peter 2:11-12).

See? Your actions can do just as much to spread the gospel as your mouth.

And here's the thing: God thinks you're awesome. He loves you like crazy, and there's not a thing you can do to take away that love, as stated in Romans 8:38-39: "I'm absolutely convinced that nothing — nothing living or dead, angelic or demonic, today or tomorrow, high or low, thinkable or unthinkable — absolutely nothing can get between us and God's love because of the way that Jesus our Master has embraced us."

His love is so rich and deep and just and pure that you cannot make Him not love you.

That is what you are: You are loved by God. You are worth something because He said you're worth something. In fact, you aren't just worth something — you're worth *everything*.

I'M ON THE OUTSIDE. DOES THAT MEAN I'M REALLY JUST IN MY OWN CLIQUE? HOW CAN I FEEL LIKE I BELONG WITHOUT GIVING UP WHO I AM?

Remember that scene in *Napoleon Dynamite* when Napoleon, Deb, and Pedro are at "the dance" and the music swells and they turn and look at all the other people dancing while they just stand on the outskirts of the dance floor, doing nothing?

I think we all feel like that sometimes. We all have
those moments in life when we feel like we're on the outside looking in, that we're standing on the edge of the dance floor
while the rest of the world cuts a rug to the smooth sounds of the
latest one-hit wonder.

Those feelings are normal.

The idea of popularity, or even just feeling as though you
belong—the whole idea of family—is a big one to God. Huge,
even. We all want to feel like we belong to something larger than
ourselves. That's why there's so much imagery in the Bible about
the body of Christ, and community, and working together to produce bigger results.

> "I moved into the city where I live when I was a
> freshman. I moved in with my dad, and my mom still
> lives in the city where I used to live. I still have
> some friends from my old city, and looking back,
> I was a completely different person when I lived
> there. I didn't like myself at all. Now I've made an
> effort to change that, and it's really helped. I don't
> try to change who I am to please people anymore."
> —Kaitlin, 17

Solitary just isn't how we're meant to roll. Look at Jesus: He
went around with twelve other dudes. The only times He went
off by Himself were times of prayer, and even then He wasn't
alone—He was with God.

So this feeling we share, the feeling of wanting to belong to
something—that's a godly, biblical feeling. We each have a part
in this world, a tiny piece of the grand mosaic that is existence,

 and we long to be put in our place, so to speak. And God is the one who does that, who guides us to the exact spot we need to occupy in order to produce His grander piece of art.

But what do you do when you aren't in that spot? If you don't mind me mixing my metaphors, what do you do when you feel like a square peg and the rest of the world is one big round hole? How can you feel like you fit without hitting up the lathe and getting your square edges rounded off?

These are really difficult questions to answer. I can't really point you in the exact direction, but I can direct you down the general path you need to travel. Will you take that?

It's a path labeled "prayer."

In our desire to fit in, there's a huge temptation to change ourselves just to gain that feeling of belonging. Or not even change ourselves—just fudge the details. How many times has this happened to you? You're in a conversation with someone you don't know too well, but you think you could probably dig as a friend, and they mention some band you've never heard of, like, "So, I got the new album today by the Tortilla Saints. [pause] You know them, right?" And instead of saying, "The *what* Saints?" you say, "Oh yeah. Good stuff," and hope they move on quickly.

I can't tell you how many times I've pulled that one.

It's just that desire to connect, to be in agreement, that makes my tiny fib seem okay. And it happens so quickly, and then it's done, and I can't go back and say, "Actually, I've never heard of them before," because then that makes me look even stupider.

Another example: You're in an unfamiliar setting, with some new people who could wind up being friends, and then they start talking about some girl who isn't there, and suddenly the speech is getting less than holy. But instead of calling it quits or encouraging the group to focus on this girl's better qualities, you chime in with opinions of your own or just sit there quietly and listen, hoping they move on quickly so you can move past this uncomfortable moment and get back to thinking you could wind up being friends.

We all have moments of weakness where we say or do something (or nothing) to fit in. Yes, they happen. But that doesn't make them right.

> "If I change who I am when I get around other people, then I assume those other people are doing it as well. I'm a pretty normal person, and if I'm doing something that ridiculous, what's to stop other people from doing it too?" — Tyler, 17

So how can you fit in without changing who you are? It all starts with realizing exactly who you are — you are God's "cherished personal treasure" (Deuteronomy 14:2). You are His before you are anything else, and so you must live your life accordingly.

I'm not saying you have to carry a Bible everywhere you go or be one of those in-your-face people who bashes everyone over the head with their faith. You don't have to stroll into every social situation with your spiritual chest thrust out like some sort of proud fighting bird, daring all those inferior sinners to tussle with you, for you will smack them into submission using only your vast debating talent and a handful of well-chosen Bible verses.

Please don't! I don't want you to do that at all. I doubt God does either.

The best thing I can tell you is to model Jesus. He didn't always fit in everywhere He went — sometimes He went very much against the grain. He wasn't always welcome, but you know what? He always brought love into every situation. Sometimes that love looked like healing, sometimes it looked like rebuke, sometimes it looked like a braided piece of leather and a bunch of overturned tables.

But it was always love.

And that's how you can fit in. Jesus didn't adjust Himself to the world—He brought love, and the world adjusted to Him.

This is the best thing you can do: Bring love. Bring forgiveness. Bring grace. Bring mercy. Bring justice. Bring righteousness.

Bring Jesus.

I THINK I MIGHT BE GAY. WHAT DO I DO ABOUT IT?

"I don't think any sect of people deals with homosexuality correctly. It makes me mad. I had a friend who was kind of feminine, and even in kindergarten he was made fun of for it. He was made fun of by all the people who were supposed to love him. He wasn't accepted by the people who were supposed to accept him. And so if he has on one hand these Christians who are making fun of him and on the other hand the homosexual community saying, 'We accept you,' which way is he going to go? He's going to go to the place where he's accepted. We don't ever want to deal with it, we don't ever want to talk about it, but we'll laugh at homosexuals and say to keep them away." — Haden, 16

If I had to point to one thing that Christians have gotten completely and utterly wrong in the past twenty years or so, it'd have to be the way we've treated homosexuality. We've treated it as this weirdo, stigmatized thing that was icky and gross. While our culture marches on under a banner of equality and such, the church has stood by and pointed fingers and called names and basically said, "You're *gay*? Go somewhere else."

Here's the thing: Homosexuality is a sin, plain and simple. The Bible puts it this way, in Romans 1:26-27: "Refusing to know God, they soon didn't know how to be human either—women didn't know how to be women, men didn't know how to be men. Sexually confused, they abused and defiled one another, women with women, men with men—all lust, no love. And then they paid for it, oh, how they paid for it—emptied of God and love, godless and loveless wretches."

Yep. It's definitely a sin.

And so is adultery. And so is stealing. And so is lying. And so is greed. And so is vanity. And so is lust. And so is using God's name in vain. And so is . . .

Look, let's break this down to brass tacks. Sin is anything that comes between you and God. It is selfishness. God is love, and the opposite of love is self. Anytime you choose to do your own thing over God's thing, you're sinning, whether that's murdering someone or holding in bitterness and unforgiveness or giving in to homosexual tendencies.

Sin is sin.

"It really bugs me that you're some sort of leper if you struggle with homosexuality. It's almost the unforgivable sin, so people who struggle with it feel like they can't struggle with it and be forgiven. And all the jokes we make about it really upset me. It's just another thing that people deal with—why do you have to treat it like it's something totally different? Why can't we be there for each other and help each other through it instead of condemning?" —Hanna, 16

The Bible also tells us that sin is in our nature. The apostle Paul struggled with this at length, telling us in the book of Romans, "If I know the law but still can't keep it, and if the power of sin within me keeps sabotaging my best intentions, I obviously need help! I realize that I don't have what it takes. I can will it, but I can't *do* it. I decide to do good, but I don't *really* do it; I decide not to do bad, but then I do it anyway. My decisions, such as they are, don't result in actions. Something has gone wrong deep within me and gets the better of me every time" (7:17-20).

Makes life sound pointless, right? But take a look at the way Paul continues in the next chapter: "With the arrival of Jesus, the Messiah, that fateful dilemma is resolved. Those who enter into Christ's being-here-for-us no longer have to live under a continuous, low-lying black cloud. A new power is in operation. The Spirit of life in Christ, like a strong wind, has magnificently cleared the air, freeing you from a fated lifetime of brutal tyranny at the hands of sin and death."

Did you catch that? It's pointless when we try on our own not to sin, but when we invite Jesus into the situation, we find freedom. And that's freedom from *all* sins, not just the glamorous ones.

Let's be honest, there's a lot about homosexuality our culture has gotten wrong, but I think one thing that's right is this: You are, in a sense, born with it. We are all born bent toward specific sins. I personally don't struggle with thievery. I don't constantly battle an inner compulsion to steal things.

"It's so easy to stereotype people — like to look at the way a guy stands and say, 'Oh, he's gay.'" — Jaime, 15

But I do have my bent: procrastination. I have a really hard time staying on task, and I'll be much more likely to read sports columns on the internet than work on, say, this book. Now, this isn't a high-profile sin, but it's a sin, nonetheless, and something I take to the Lord with frequency.

If you're experiencing homosexual tendencies, you're simply discovering your personal bent. Turns out your bent is one that people are much more opinionated about.

But what to do about it? This is where the rubber meets the road. For starters, let me tell you this: God loves you, and you aren't anything but loved by Him. No matter how people treat you, you are loved. Remember that.

Second, you need to make a decision to take this sin to God—to openly and honestly let Him into that part of your heart, willing to accept the consequences of that action. He knows best, and, as we just learned from Paul, He's the only way to freedom.

Third, know that you don't have to carry this weight by yourself. That's completely the wrong way to go about it. Pray, pray, pray, asking God to point you to someone you can trust, someone who can help you live the life you want to live.

And this doesn't apply just to homosexuality. It applies to *all* sin. Accountability is the best way to deal with it, to get on the road to recovery and that free life Paul talks about in Romans. Seek accountability. It's the first step on that road.

CHAPTER 2

YOU AND YOUR FAMILY

Children, do what your parents tell you. This delights the Master no end. (Colossians 3:20)

Parents, don't come down too hard on your children or you'll crush their spirits. (Colossians 3:21)

Long, long ago he decided to adopt us into his family through Jesus Christ. (What pleasure he took in planning this!) (Ephesians 1:5)

DO I REALLY HAVE TO LOVE MY PARENTS? AREN'T THEY JUST OUT TO GET ME, OR DO THEY ACTUALLY LOVE ME BACK?

The word *family* is an important one to God. The Bible is riddled with family imagery, much of it pertaining to the way we as Christians have become part of God's family. Christianity itself is based on the idea of family — God wanted to build a family, and He built it through adoption. He adopted me and (hopefully) you.

> "Parental **influence helps** you choose **better friends** and **make better choices."** — Michael, 17

So family is a big deal to God. It's a tangible way we experience His love here on earth, believe it or not. Because in a family, at least the way God designed it, you get to practice (and receive) mercy and grace. You get to discover what it's really like to screw up over and over again, only to run into a brick wall of unconditional love. You learn how to treat the other members of your family the same way.

At least that's how it's supposed to be. But, humans being humans, we've also discovered about a zillion ways to mess that up: divorce, sexual/physical/emotional abuse, cold shoulders, purposeless rebellion, dumb things said in the heat of an argument . . . the list goes on and on. We're very good at inventing new ways of destroying the marvelous picture God drew to show us what He's all about. Of course, the Devil helps us, but so many of us willingly let him do it.

So we stumble through this thing called life, trying to get everyone else to see things *our* way. And since we're with our family members most of the time, we tend to take most of our junk out on them. Or we just keep our junk inside and act happy while we're at home, waiting until we're with our friends to get out our frustrations, maybe not in the healthiest ways.

What's the solution? God says it's love. At the risk of sounding like the lyrics to a cheesy power ballad, you have to believe in the power of love. (Actually, I'm pretty sure those *are* the lyrics to a cheesy power ballad.)

We're called to love each other. Love isn't a feeling you feel—it's a decision you make. You consciously decide to love, regardless of the circumstances. Whether your parents are married or divorced, whether you have a single parent or multiple stepparents, whether you live in complete freedom or with different rules for different houses, the principle of love is a blanket principle that always applies.

"My parents just got **divorced** last year, so I **had both** of them most of my **life.** But I can **see how** it's harder on my younger brother and sister, that my brother doesn't have that fatherly influence in his life, and how my sister was a real daddy's girl and now doesn't have that. It's been a lot harder for them, and it would be easier for them if they had both parents."
—Jennifer, 17

You may live in complete luxury or utter despair, with a loving family or with a family that is nothing but falling apart. God sees you and has one command: Love. Seriously.

Again, an easy thing to say, not so easy to do.

And you know what? I don't really have any practical pointers on this one, other than to say this: If you're having trouble loving, quit trying on your own and let God do it through you. Seek Him. Ask Him for help.

If you've been abused, or are being abused in any way, seek help. Go to someone you can trust. Tell someone. There are thousands of places where you can get help; you just have to ask for it. God will always provide it — maybe not in the way you're looking for it, but He will. He's faithful like that.

WHAT DO I DO WHEN I GET SICK OF MY PARENTS?

Let's talk about your family. I'm going to go out on a limb here and say that your family is the *only* screwed-up family in the world. Right? No one else's parents are as embarrassing as yours, no one else's brother or sister is as frustrating, no one else's aunts/uncles/cousins are as annoying at Thanksgiving. Nope. In fact, I've spoken with all the other families out there, and we've all agreed: *Your* family? They're the champs.

Wait. Maybe that's *my* family I'm talking about. Because I'll tell you, my family embarrassed the heck out of me when I was in high school. That was about the time my straight-laced dad discovered shorts. He'd worn pants (not jeans, not khakis — poly/cotton pants) his *entire life.* I'll never forget the summer he came home in these gray shorts that made him look like the back half of a stumpy elephant.

See, because before he discovered those shorts, he had the pants. And the pants masked a horrible, horrible fact: Every pair of socks he owned was black. Every. Single. One. My dad was fond of cramming his black-socked feet into those canvas shoes you can get at Kmart or Wal-Mart, those slip-on numbers that come clipped together with a hook between them so they can hang on a peg in the store. You know the ones I mean?

And that was just the lower half. The top was complemented—always—by a short-sleeve dress shirt, an enormous, fake-leather eyeglasses holder in the pocket (that became a pocket protector in later years so he could tote around a ballpoint pen and mechanical pencil), and a newsboy cap perched precariously atop his head like a cherry on a sundae. And this was *well* before newsboy caps were ever cool (remember those thirty seconds?).

So. Yeah. Embarrassing dad. And this is how he would dress in our suburban paradise. Did I *ever* want my dad around when my friends would come over? Heck no. Because though he looked uncool, he *acted* even worse. He was a big fan of the pun, or the play on words. He was marvelously clever, but not very silly (it wasn't until I became an adult that I appreciated his sense of humor). I cringed anytime he opened his mouth around one of my friends, afraid that some zinger would come out and then drop to the floor with a leaden clunk.

And as far as outward love toward me, his youngest son? Well, he was terrible at that. Just terrible. He said "I love you" to me one time in my teens. One time. I was the youngest kid in my class, so young I wasn't eligible to take my driver's test until midway through my junior year. I passed the written exam with flying colors and started passing the driving exam like a Ferrari on the Daytona Motor Speedway.

I was doing awesome. Using my blinkers, applying the perfect amount of pressure to the brake, obeying posted speed limits, checking my mirrors—even parallel parking like a pro.

Until the Driving Test Lady told me to back in a straight line.

I had no idea this would be on the test, so I hadn't even practiced it. I didn't think it could be too hard, so I gave it a shot and wound up going more in the sort of line you'd expect from a moth in the backyard at night. That is, nothing close to straight.

So I failed my test, and that was hard. I was a Test Master. I always did well on tests, and this one should've been no different.

> "My parents refuse to separate themselves from our lives. They don't take the attitude of 'We're the parents and you're the kids.' And from talking to my friends, it seems like my relationship with my parents is kind of strange, because I talk to them all the time. About everything. I don't ever think, 'Oh, they're just my parents—they won't understand me.'"—Haden, 16

That was a hard drive back to school, and my dad was quiet the whole time. He knew I was the youngest kid in my class; all my friends had their licenses, and now I was going to have to go back in there and tell them I'd failed. I'll admit it—I started to cry.

I don't know if it was the tears or what, but my father, a man who was by turns stern and jovial, reached a hand out, placed it on my shoulder, and said, "It's okay, son. I love you."

I held that against my dad for a long time. Seems weird, doesn't it? To hold that against him? The one time he'd actually shown me, verbally, his love? But it was precisely because of that—precisely because he'd *never* done it before and never did it again while I was a teenager.

That was how my dad screwed it up. As I got older, and as he got sick, I began to realize how much he loved me, had always loved me. He just didn't know how to say it—for him, it was hard. For whatever reason, he just wasn't vocal about it. Instead, he showed me his love by providing for me and my brother and my mom. And by making sure we were spiritually solid through taking us to church and through teaching us about God at home.

Fortunately I realized all this stuff before he died. I talked to him about it, there in the hospital actually, terrified that I wouldn't get through it before he passed, scared to death that I wouldn't see any of my bitterness resolved until we met in heaven.

So why am I telling you all this stuff about my dad? I want you to take it easy on your parents because I'm pretty sure that in their hearts they really love you and want what's best for you. I know this isn't the case for everyone, but I'm willing to bet it's the case for you.

Your parents love you. Trust me — from a parent who often messes up when trying to show my kids how I love them. It's true. Boil out all the frustrated behavior and raised voices (oh, like *you* never talk back — come on) and hands thrown up in the air and allowances docked and groundings and all that other stuff and you'll come down to this: love.

> "I almost **wish** my **family** had a **problem, because** that's **the** norm. **When** I **bring friends** over or talk to friends about their families, I almost **feel guilty** about **being** so **lucky** to **have** a family that's tight-knit and that gets along for the most part. I **wish** I could take everyone who doesn't have that experience into my house and say, 'You're okay now.'" — Kat, 17

That's just the way God set it up. He wants to show you His love, but He uses other people to do that. I don't know why He decides to tote around His love in busted-up buckets (see 2 Corinthians 4:7), but that's the way He wants it, so we have to trust that it's the best way.

I JUST WANT MY PARENTS TO LET ME LIVE MY LIFE. HOW DO I GET MY INDEPENDENCE AND SHOW THEM HOW GROWN-UP I AM?

This one's pretty simple, really.

You want independence? Show yourself to be trustworthy with smaller stuff, and your parents will trust you with bigger stuff.

Like I said, pretty simple.

If you want to, say, hang out with your friends every night, but always come home a half hour after curfew, your parents probably aren't going to let you keep hanging out.

If you want to, say, decorate your own room, but constantly leave it a mess, with clothes on the floor, two-month-old bowls of cereal on the dresser, and leaky fast-food drink cups piled above the rim of the trash can, your parents probably aren't going to give you permission to bust out the paintbrush.

I believe you are on your way to adulthood but still need to learn a few things on the way there. And one of those things is a little something called responsibility. But the trick with responsibility is this: You have to be responsible with everything, not just the stuff you *want* to be responsible with.

Who knows—maybe your parents are the types of parents who give you pretty much everything you want, regardless of how you treat it. Maybe you're really responsible with your stuff, but have parents who can't afford to give you anything more (as was the case with my teenage years). Regardless of your situation, God has something to say about it.

In Luke 16:10-12, Jesus breaks the whole concept of responsibility down to its bare essence: "If you're honest in small things, you'll be honest in big things; if you're a crook in small things, you'll be a crook in big things. If you're not honest in small jobs, who will put you in charge of the store?"

See the connection there? The way you treat the small stuff is the way you'll treat the big stuff.

And this doesn't go for stuff, either. Jesus is constantly on us about our perception of the world around us, constantly reminding us not to get too big for our britches. We are not the be-all/end-all of the world; it does not exist solely for us — we're only a part of it, just like everyone else.

Perhaps this is why Jesus encourages us to treat even the poorest individuals like royalty. In Matthew 25:35-36, He talks about doing kind things for hurting people in our society: for the hungry, the thirsty, the poor, the unclothed, the homeless. Jesus tells us we need to take care of them, meet their needs, and then He says, in verse 40, "I'm telling the solemn truth: Whenever you did one of these things to someone overlooked or ignored, that was me — you did it to me."

So apparently Jesus is interested in the way we treat the world around us, especially when we start looking down our noses at parts of that world. And I think this has less to do with the world and more to do with you. You as an individual. The way you look at the world. It seems to me that Jesus is saying, "Don't be so full of yourself that you think you can treat the world like trash — you're a part of it, just like everyone else, and if you trash it, you're trashing Me. You're trashing My name."

The cool thing about that passage in Matthew is the way it begins. Jesus is talking to the people who did the little things, who took care of the little people, and He says, in verse 34, "The King will say to those on his right, 'Enter, you who are blessed by my Father! Take what's coming to you in this kingdom. It's been ready for you since the world's foundation.'"

He's talking about heaven.

The people who treat the world kindly are the ones who are rewarded. So when we talk about responsibility, there are much bigger things at stake than just tending to your room—it's about tending to your worldview, about taking care of the world around you and trusting God to reward you when the time is right.

HOW DO I HANDLE MY PARENTS' DIVORCE?

"My dad is getting ready to go through a second divorce, and I'm going to be the one that's affected by it the most. And that's happened my whole life. I haven't done anything to my parents, I haven't been the cause of anything, but I've always been the one that's most affected by it. It really upsets me. But the whole family thing doesn't really work for me."
—Kaitlin, 17

As you may have noticed, throughout this book I've included quotes from students from different walks of life. When I was doing the interviews with those students, one of them, Kat, told me a great story that was too long for a quote but that I felt needed to be included.

One summer, Kat and her mother visited a summer camp in the country, a remote place that was located about an hour away from her hometown. As they got in the car to drive home, a butterfly landed on it. They started the drive, and Kat watched this butterfly hold on for dear life, just waiting for it to flutter away on its own or be ripped from the vehicle by the force of the wind.

But it never went anywhere. It stayed, stuck to the car, for an hour.

As they got into the city, they reached a fairly heavily trafficked intersection and the butterfly decided it had come to the end of the line. With a beat of its wings, it took off from the car and landed on a nearby sidewalk.

"Look, Mom," Kat said. "We had a real impact on that butterfly's life. It completely changed."

Somewhere around the word *changed*, a bird came out of nowhere, plucked the butterfly up in its beak, and flew away, presumably to feed its baby chicks in a nest somewhere.

Kat, naturally, burst into tears at the thought of this butterfly having gone through so much only to wind up as dinner.

But her mother decided to point out that from the bird's point of view, that butterfly was a blessing—a meal delivery to feed its family, brought from an hour away.

When it comes to divorce, it's easy to feel like that butterfly, isn't it? You didn't *ask* to be pecked; you were just doing what you could to hold on as the winds of a turbulent life whistled around your ears.

It's also easy to think of the bird as the villain in that story, because I told it from the point of view of the butterfly. But the bird was just doing what God created it to do—snap up insects and feed its family. To seize opportunity wherever it might find it.

So what do you do when your parents make your life messy and hard by divorcing? You become the bird. You look for blessings wherever they might be, even if they're in strange places where you don't expect to see them—like a country butterfly on a city sidewalk. And when you see those blessings, you snap them up.

What could those blessings be? Friends. Siblings. Teachers.

The Bible. A praise and worship song that touches that secret part of your heart you don't show to anyone.

Jesus.

God. The Father.

Someday, when you have kids, you'll gain a greater understanding of God as your Father. I didn't get it until after I had kids, anyway. Your earthly parents are *always* going to let you down, no matter what. You could romanticize and fantasize all you want about the perfect family, but it doesn't exist—your parents are still humans who make mistakes.

> "I regret the way my parents handled raising me and my sister after they divorced. They changed so quickly. They ripped us out of everything we knew. I automatically felt like I had to take care of my little sister. And my dad has money, and that's the way he shows his affection, so it was never 'I'm going to be here for you'; it was 'Here, I'm going to hand you money and you can go do whatever you want with it and have fun.' I hated that."
> —Kaitlin, 17

That's why God wants to be your Father. He isn't safe, He isn't waiting to take your order so you can get whatever you want—He's a loving Father who knows how to take care of His kids, no matter what.

Turn to Him. Ask Him to help you find the blessings, the butterflies, you need to sustain you in this moment. You never know where they'll be.

Thanks for the story, Kat.

DO I HAVE TO HANG OUT WITH MY FAMILY?

"When I was about seven, my parents got divorced, and I haven't really seen much of my dad since then. And today, my brother, my mom, and I are the trifecta of terror — we're so bonded together. We're never mad at each other for more than a couple of hours. It just doesn't happen. I'm sure God would've wanted my dad to stick around, but He made the most of this situation, and this way of living seems pretty awesome to me." — Grant, 17

Not too long ago, my wife and I started a tradition in our household. Every Sunday night, my wife makes homemade pizza (or, if we don't have those particular ingredients, throws a bag of pizza rolls in the oven), pops some popcorn, and throws out some fruit (so we can have *something* healthy). Then everyone in the family plops down in front of the TV for Family Movie Night.

Now, most of my kids are young, so they tend to watch a little more television than the rest of us (we're cracking down on it though). But no matter how much they watch throughout the week, they're always excited for Family Movie Night. Even our fifteen-year-old digs it. It's something that everyone in our family looks forward to because even though we're together at different times during the week, we know for a fact that this time, the evening of Sunday, is unshakeable. We *will* have Family Movie Night.

Why is this time so important to us, to me? I didn't grow up in a real close-knit family. I loved my parents and my brother, sure, but I never wanted to spend time with them. I always preferred to be in my room reading or listening to music or working on a jigsaw puzzle or practicing my juggling skills (sadly, I really did that—but as a result, I know how to juggle!).

I never spent any real time with my family, except at mealtimes and in the car on the way to church. Twice a year, we loaded up and headed to Dallas to visit my grandmother, but even then, I just did the same things I did in my room (well, reading and listening to music—puzzles require a table, and I never got the nerve to whip out the ol' juggling clubs in the backseat of our car).

As a result, my family and I aren't that close. My father has since passed away, and our relationship got stronger the closer he came to death, but even then, we weren't super-tight like I am with my own kids. I email my mom frequently but rarely ever see her, and my brother lives about a thousand miles away, which makes it difficult to maintain close contact with him.

I'm not telling you all this to make you feel sorry for me—quite the opposite. I have a rich family life now because I'm consciously choosing to invest in it, every week, every day.

Whether you like them or not, these people are your family—and they will never *not* be your family. Even after they're dead and gone, you will define them by the link they have to you as your family. Your parents will always be your parents. Your siblings will always be your siblings. I always introduce my brother as "my brother Randy." I never say, "This is some guy I know; his name is Randy. And also, as a little factoid, we are related biologically, in that we sprang from the same mother."

"My brother is seven years older than me. And so growing up, I was always this sort of annoying brat to him, and he was just this person who lived in my house. So I never really got a chance to know him. He joined the navy when I was in the eighth grade, and now he's stationed far away. Now that I am old enough to appreciate a relationship with him, he's really far away. I wish we could have a better relationship."
— Jenava, 17

So my advice? Spend time with them, no matter how boring or annoying you find it. You won't always be this way — someday you'll be all grown up and you'll need to count on someone in your family, and you want to make sure they're there for you. And you want to make sure they know you'll be there for them. It never hurts to invest in people.

MY PARENTS' RULES AND CURFEWS ARE LAME. WHAT DO I DO ABOUT THAT?

You want a solid answer here? Respect them.

I knew you didn't want me to say that. I can almost hear you, with your voice going sky-high, spluttering, "But . . . !" My children do this all the time at home, so I know exactly what it sounds like.

I'm just saying: Respect the rules and curfews your folks lay down. Because if you ever want the rules to change, you have to respect them.

Ah, now we're getting somewhere.

I'm going to give you the inside scoop on the way we parents think, and I'm going to use a simple example from the life of my three-year-old daughter, just to make sure you get it.

"I'm driving now. And I'll be driving with my mom, and I'll want to take a right turn or something, and I totally think I can do it, whereas my mom will tell me to do something different. And she's been driving twenty years longer than me, so I'll take her experience over mine. It still drives me crazy, though, because I totally know I could've made that right turn." — Gabrielle, 16

The other day, as I was eating lunch, she peered at my plate and, seeing her favorite chips (Doritos, if you must know), asked if she could have some.

"Sure thing," I said, selecting a nice-sized triangle from my plate and handing it to her.

Her mouth started to turn down on the ends, and her eyebrows furrowed in sadness. "I wanted three!" she said as she started to take the chip from me.

I still had a decent grasp on that Dorito, so I delicately extracted it from her hand. "How about none?" I said. "Would you rather have none?"

Her eyebrows and mouth went back to normal. She shook her head and held out her hand to receive the original offering. Suddenly she had a thankful heart for the chip I shared, and I could see her gratitude as she munched that thing down.

So I gave her two more.

See what happened there? It's human nature that when one person is dictating the terms of something to another person and that other person goes into whine mode, the dictator will dig in his heels and become super-strict.

When your parents are giving you rules or curfews, if you

throw a big whine-fit (like a *three-year-old* would do, I might add), you don't get your point across, and you (hopefully) don't get your way. All you do is make yourself look bad and encourage your parents to withhold even more liberties from your childish self.

> "It's **usually** not **worth** talking back to **my** parents or arguing **with them,** so I just **shut up** and do **whatever** they ask." — Michael, 17

But if you respect the rules? Show gratitude for them? Now your parents see someone who is mature enough to recognize generosity where they see it, and they'll trust you with more.

This is a principle we see at work even in the Bible, where Paul says in Galatians 6:7-8, "Don't be misled: No one makes a fool of God. What a person plants, he will harvest. The person who plants selfishness, ignoring the needs of others—ignoring God!—harvests a crop of weeds. All he'll have to show for his life is weeds! But the one who plants in response to God, letting God's Spirit do the growth work in him, harvests a crop of real life, eternal life."

Do you see that? What you give is what you get. It works in life, in the larger, grander things of faith, and it works at home. If you want your parents to respect your decision making, then respect theirs.

And when you plant good things into your parents, into your family, you'll harvest good things. Simple as that.

Dorito, anyone?

WHAT DO I DO WHEN MY SIBLINGS BUG THE CRAP OUT OF ME?

"Whenever my sister, who's twelve, doesn't think she's my age, we're good." — Gabrielle, 16

It's the craziest thing—no one can frustrate you like a sibling. My brother is almost six years older than me, so we didn't relate too well to each other. We were just in different stations in life. Basically, we related to each other by fighting and, since he was so much older, him winning.

But you know how it is—your brother can pick on you all he wants (or you can pick on your brother, depending on who's the oldest), but if someone else tries to mess with you, they will incur the wrath of your sibling in a way you've never seen.

My kids are like that. They're young still, but they stick up for each other. Fiercely. When my son was five, his seven-year-old sister was getting in trouble for something at home and he actually stood between her and my wife to plead her case.

That's just the way family is supposed to be. Maybe you and your siblings don't get along. Maybe you annoy the crap out of each other most of the time. Maybe you're best friends. Whatever the case, God wants you to treat them with love and for them to love you back.

"In my experience, I'm a lot closer to my sister than I am to my parents. She's the one who sat me down last month and said, 'Hanna, you're acting differently. You're never like this. Why are you so mad at people?' She's the one who challenged me." — Hanna, 16

That doesn't mean you never fight or that you never have disagreements or get annoyed with each other. You are human, after all, and things are going to get on your nerves. The only way to be in perfect harmony at all times is to lose your individuality and personality, and that's just not going to happen.

But that's where grace and mercy come in. You get mad at each other? You work through it, realizing that, if nothing else, you're stuck with each other. Might as well make it peaceful.

CHAPTER 3

YOU AND THE PEOPLE AROUND YOU

Our people have to learn to be diligent in their work so that all necessities are met (especially among the needy) and they don't end up with nothing to show for their lives. (Titus 3:14)

Love from the center of who you are; don't fake it. Run for dear life from evil; hold on for dear life to good. Be good friends who love deeply; practice playing second fiddle. . . . Bless your enemies; no cursing under your breath. Laugh with your happy friends when they're happy; share tears when they're down. Get along with each other; don't be stuck-up. Make friends with nobodies; don't be the great somebody. (Romans 12:9-10,14-16)

If you've gotten anything at all out of following Christ, if his love has made any difference in your life, if being in a community of the Spirit means anything to you, if you have a heart, if you care—then do me a favor: Agree with each other, love each other, be deep-spirited friends. Don't push your way to the front; don't sweet-talk your way to the top. Put yourself aside, and help others get ahead. Don't be obsessed with getting your own advantage. Forget yourselves long enough to lend a helping hand. (Philippians 2:1-4)

DOES IT MATTER WHO I'M FRIENDS WITH?

Yes and no. Confused yet?

> "People hate to not have fun. If you don't have any friends, you can't have fun, so sometimes people go outside of themselves to get friends. I couldn't go through school without any friends. I'd just sit at home doing nothing." — Andrew, 16

This is one of those answers that depends on the *real* question being asked, which breaks down like this: Do you want to be friends with someone because you think they're cool and you want to, in a sense, emulate them, or are you hoping to introduce them to the gospel?

Do you want to influence or to *be* influenced?

This is a situation where you really need to check your heart, because the answer reveals a lot about your true motives, and this is an area that could go either way.

I'll give you some examples. In the Old Testament, the Israelites kept straying from God specifically because they

associated with idol worshippers. They started copy-
ing the worship methods of the nations around them
and it got them off track so badly that they got
invaded and captured.

On the other hand, 1 Samuel 20 tells us about two of the
greatest friends of all time, David and Jonathan. These guys
looked out for each other through thick and thin and had a major
common bond: They both served God.

The Israelites were influenced by idol worshippers and
became idol worshippers.

David and Jonathan influenced each other and became the
most celebrated friendship in the Bible.

The thing about friendship is this: Your friends should make
you a better person, and you should make *them* better people. It
is a two-way street, in a sense, so you want to make sure you're
going down that street and sharing your life with people who are
putting something positive into it.

> "**Even if** you're a **really independent person, you
> always have** to **have someone else.** You **always
> have** to **be accepted.** Maybe not **by the world** or **by
> every single person, but you** can't **survive with-
> out friends. And some people** take **really drastic
> measures to be** accepted — and are not **themselves."**
> — Jenava, 17

Now, there's a big difference between friends and acquain-
tances, so there should be a big difference in how you should
choose them. I want to make sure to stress something here: I don't
believe you are called to associate exclusively with Christians.
Jesus was very plain in His parting words to the disciples that we

are to interact with the world, to bring the message of Christ to people who need to hear it:
"Go out and train everyone you meet, far and
near, in this way of life" (Matthew 28:19).

We are clearly not supposed to hole up and interact only with
Christians. But we are not to go into the world and suddenly act
worldly, either. We are to be "a breath of fresh air" (Philippians
2:14) in the world without letting the pollution of sin infect us.

We need to set the tempo of the world around us. I'm a musi-
cian, and when I play in a band setting, I always pay close attention to the drummer because he's the one setting the tempo for
the rest of us. If the rest of the band tries to do its own thing or
tries to sway the band to *their* tempo, the song becomes a mess.
The drummer is the one with the guiding authority to keep the
band on track.

You need to be the drummer of your life. You need to be the
drummer of your world.

> "Regardless of who you're with, you should always be
> respectful. My mom always says, 'You don't have to be
> friends, but you do have to be friendly.' It's so hard to
> do, but you have to try." — Kat, 17

You need to set the tempo. Interact with others, welcome
them into what you're doing, but don't let them take over the
song. Don't let them force their tempo on you. Don't let their
behavior influence yours.

Influence *them*.

WHAT IS THE OPPOSITE SEX REALLY THINKING? DO I WANT THEM TO NOTICE ME?

> "There's this author I love, but she always writes these books about kids falling in love, and it's a happy ending — but that's not real. You get that fairy-tale mindset very early, but it isn't real."
> — Kaitlin, 17

Most likely, they're thinking the same thing you're thinking: "Oh, man. I'm so nervous!" You are at a time of your life where parts of you have awakened that you didn't even know existed. It is a time of giddiness, a feeling that a vast, unexplored country lies before you, and, since you don't know exactly what it will be like, you're wrestling with both excitement and terror.

Mostly terror.

But the great thing is, whomever you're interested in is probably wrestling with excitement and mostly terror as well. So that's great news for the both of you.

Now, here's where I'm going to make you mad.

I want you to listen to the terror.

Look, life is complicated enough at your age for you to deal with the pressures of having a boyfriend/girlfriend. You already have a zillion other things going on that are challenging your ability to keep your emotions in check — why give yourself *another* challenge?

"Your life should be intentional. There should be reasons behind everything you do, which is why I don't date. It's not just that my parents say I can't—there's just so much crap I'm going to have to go through in life. Why add something like dating that is completely unnecessary? I don't condemn those who do date, but personally I don't want to do it."—Haden, 16

I don't want to sound tragically unhip or uncool or whatever word you might throw at me, but it really is pretty liberating not to have a significant other at this stage of your life. Yes, it can be fun, to a degree, but the stresses that come with the desire of wanting a boyfriend/girlfriend, let alone maintaining a relationship, far outweigh that fun.

Does that mean you can't hang out with members of the opposite sex? Of course not. I'm simply suggesting that you keep your own heart and mind in check, to make sure you're focusing as much as you can on your family, school, and God—and not in that order.

Trust me on this one. It won't be forever—you'll be able to date soon enough. But going against the grain and steering clear of romantic relationships is one of the best things you can do for your high school experience.

How do I know? Because it worked for me. Now, I *wanted* to have a girlfriend when I was in high school—I wanted it desperately, actually (probably most of the girls I knew could smell the desperation, which is why they steered clear). But I could never get past the "friend" barrier with a girl, and in retrospect I'm glad I didn't. My mind was distracted enough with all the school stuff, and youth group stuff, and all that—I honestly didn't have time for a girlfriend.

I had time to *like* girls, of course. And I'm not saying you can't like people. If you like 'em, you like 'em. I guess I'm just trying to help you keep your heart in check. This thing called "perspective" is so essential to making it through your high school experience with a minimum amount of scarring.

So what if all your friends have relationships? So what if you really think you're missing out? I'm telling you—you're not. You get into a relationship at this time in your life and you're asking for a harder road to walk.

> **"There's pressure to date. If you don't have a relationship, people think you're doing something wrong. I don't have a boyfriend and people ask me all the time what I'm doing wrong. I don't think I'm doing anything wrong." — Kaitlin, 17**

You aren't going to die if you don't have a boyfriend. Going through high school with no girlfriend is not going to cause your eyeballs to fall out of your head. All that's going to happen is this: You're going to make it through high school with less stress, and then you're going to move on to something resembling adulthood, which is the best time to do the relationship stuff, after you have some more mature legs underneath you.

You have enough to do just figuring out who you are—deal with that first. See, you're in this precious time of life right now. You're bridging the gap between kidhood and adulthood, and during that gap, you're trying on a lot of different hats. You're going through phases of interest, phases of fashion, maybe even phases of personality. You are in the worst possible position to find a long-term, meaningful relationship that will last a lifetime.

> "I think it's important to date. I think it's important to be well-rounded by having different relationships. I think the reason relationships fail a lot of times is because you sort of put that person on a pedestal, and when that person falls, it hurts really bad. That's why I say to have relationships, but keep it casual. And having small, casual relationships will help you decide what you want." — Alex, 17

So if that's the case, why date? You only open yourself up to some serious temptations that will get you nowhere. Instead, hang out in groups. Just be friends with your friends, even friends who might seem a little more special than others. If it's meant to turn into something grander, it will *still* be meant to turn into something grander after you graduate.

Patience is a tough thing to develop, especially in the area of relationships. But it's something you will thank yourself for later down the road. Trust me, as a married guy with an awesome wife and six kids who never even kissed a girl until he was twenty years old (and even then it was the woman he eventually married) — God can do anything.

WHAT'S THE DEAL WITH SEX? IS EVERYONE REALLY DOING IT?

Wherever you are, I want you to do something.

I want you to put this book down for a second and look all around you, 360 degrees.

Did you do it yet?

Come on, I mean it. Do it.

Okay, welcome back. Thanks for indulging me. So, what'd you see?

I'm willing to guess you saw at least one thing with some sort of sexual or sensual connotation to it.

"Sex," as the advertising industry likes to call it, is everywhere. Of course, we aren't really seeing sex in all the ads and signs and sitcoms and PG-13 movies and album covers and music videos and YouTube videos. Nope. What we're seeing is lust, and that, my friends, is bad news.

Sex has become this almost mystical object in our culture. This is where the Devil has really made a lot of progress, turning sex into this golden ring to be possessed—and since a good 99.9% of us have functioning equipment, and a desire to use it, we're all in a good condition to get wrapped up in sex and lust.

> **"There's** no reason to **put yourself in a bad situation by dating.** Your body's already screaming, 'Physical! Physical! Sex! Sex!' If you don't want to look at bad things on the internet, you just don't look at it, you block it, whatever. This is the same thing. If you don't want to be in a sexual relationship before you're married, the best way is not to have a relationship beyond friendship with someone."**—** Haden, 16

The Bible is very clear about sex, and you've probably heard a million youth group sermons on this, but I'm going to give you one more.

For the specifics of what "sex" means, check out the answer to the question "What is sex, really? How do I define it?" (See page **68**.) For now, let's talk about this common notion that if you don't at least experiment a little, you'll be left out of what everyone else is doing.

It doesn't matter whether "everyone is doing it."

As Christians, we're called to a higher standard. Deuteronomy 14:2 says, "You only are a people holy to GOD, your God; GOD chose you out of all the people on Earth as his cherished personal treasure." God was talking about the Israelites there, but the sentiment holds for all Christians in 1 Peter 2:9: "You are the ones chosen by God, chosen for the high calling of priestly work, chosen to be a holy people, God's instruments to do his work and speak out for him."

In the King James Version of the Bible, in both of those verses, the words *cherished personal treasure* and *God's instruments* are translated as the word *peculiar*.

> "A couple of girls I've liked have expected me to want a physical relationship, even though I don't. So it went to these weird extremes, where they would ask if I wanted to be physical, and I'd say, 'No.' I had to sever all ties with them because they were so awkward about it." — Tyler, 17

You're *supposed* to go against the grain. You're supposed to flip our culture upside down. You're supposed to be different from everyone else. Not in that sense where they're all, "What a weirdo." The ideal way to be different is to live to a higher standard, where people look at you and think, *Man, there's something different about that person — and I want it.*

HOW FAR IS "TOO FAR," ANYWAY?

So let's say you're in a relationship with someone. And you're trying to keep it clean, but you want to have a little fun, and holding hands is nice, but kissing is nicer, and . . . then what? Where should you draw the line?

"I think dating is very, very personal. It's a maturity deal, and I think 90 percent of kids aren't ready to handle it. I went out with someone for just short of a year, and it was not a bad experience at all. We were just like best friends. We still are. But even so, I think I'm not ready to date. There's weird stuff that happens when you're alone—it's just too easy for it to become a bad situation."—Grant, 17

In my opinion, you should've drawn the line about three steps ago. Look, sin isn't something we can just dink around with. You have to be on guard, all the time, because the journey from thought to desire to action is a surprisingly short one.

And it's an inborn thing. You're at constant war with sin, whether you like it or not. Jesus is the only person who's been completely free of sin, so if you think *you* can do it, you're fooling yourself into thinking you're equal with God Himself. Take a look at James 1:14-15: "The temptation to give in to evil comes from us and only us. We have no one to blame but the leering, seducing flare-up of our own lust. Lust gets pregnant, and has a baby: sin! Sin grows up to adulthood, and becomes a real killer."

See? Sin comes from within, but only through a little manipulation from our enemy, the Devil. And in 1 Peter 5:8, we read, "Keep a cool head. Stay alert. The Devil is poised to pounce, and would like nothing better than to catch you napping." He's just waiting on you to let your guard down in the area of temptation so he can pounce on you and drag you to a place you'd never imagine having gone in the first place.

Have you ever been lost? Like really, really lost, maybe in the woods or on a road trip? You know

that awful time when you come to the realization that you have
no idea where you are? That doesn't happen right away. The first
wrong turn isn't the one that gets you lost — it's just the one that
starts you down the road to lostness.

I'm saying not to make that first wrong turn. Keep
yourself peculiar. Keep your physical relationship with
the opposite sex on the up-and-up. If it helps, here's a little
guideline: Don't do anything you wouldn't do in front of
your entire family. Parents, siblings, grandparents, aunts,
uncles. If you couldn't do it in public, don't do it in private.

> "I've surrounded myself with friends who don't have
> sex, so I don't feel pressure to engage in physical
> activity." — Michael, 17

Even better, don't put yourself in a private situation. That's
asking for trouble. Stay with groups, and keep yourself accountable to other people.

WHAT IS SEX, REALLY? HOW DO I DEFINE IT?

Sex is a beautiful, beautiful thing that God created. It's so multi-
faceted and multilayered that I don't have time or space to discuss
it entirely. Its sheer beauty is so deep and elegant — and that's
what bugs me the most about the way our culture treats it. Instead
of the ultimate pursuit between a husband and wife, we're treating
it like some sort of goofy hobby.

I really can't think of a better way to put it than this:

There's more to sex than mere skin on skin. Sex is as
much spiritual mystery as physical fact. As written in

Scripture, "The two become one." Since we want to become spiritually one with the Master, we must not pursue the kind of sex that avoids commitment and intimacy, leaving us more lonely than ever—the kind of sex that can never "become one." There is a sense in which sexual sins are different from all others. In sexual sin we violate the sacredness of our own bodies, these bodies that were made for God-given and God-modeled love, for "becoming one" with another. Or didn't you realize that your body is a sacred place, the place of the Holy Spirit? Don't you see that you can't live however you please, squandering what God paid such a high price for? The physical part of you is not some piece of property belonging to the spiritual part of you. God owns the whole works. So let people see God in and through your body. (1 Corinthians 6:16-20)

See, God thought up sex as the ultimate picture of what we were made for. When a husband and wife engage in sex, they are recreating the blessed time when we as Christians will be reunited with Jesus in heaven (see Revelation 19:7). At the same time, the husband and wife are being bonded at a soulish level ("the two become one"), which is necessary for their success as a couple. They are giving pieces of themselves to each other—pieces they'll never get back. That's why divorce hurts so much; it's a violation of a soulish trust.

This is also why casual sex always winds up hurting the people who participate. Even though you participated halfheartedly or just for fun or because you were bored, you gave away a piece of your soul and received a piece in return. You made a bond, at the soul level, without considering it.

"The point of dating is to find your spouse, which is why I don't date in high school. This isn't the rest of my life." — Anna, 16

Forget all the dangers of sex for a moment and instead focus on this: Could it be that God limited sex to between a husband and wife not because He wanted to spoil the party but because He wanted to protect us from unimaginable hurt? Could it be for our own benefit?

Think of it like this: A steak knife is a very useful tool. It has a specific purpose. It is a good thing. But not in the hands of a child. If I give a steak knife to my three-year-old daughter, I know what to expect: She's going to stab her steak with it and attempt to eat it off the knife, and she runs the risk of being seriously hurt by it.

That doesn't mean she *will* be hurt, necessarily. She may cut herself, or she may not. Does that mean I should let her use it? No way. As a loving parent who knows that my three-year-old daughter isn't ready for the responsibility of a steak knife, I'm going to keep that thing away from her no matter how curious she might be about it or how eager she might seem to use it.

If you fool around with sex, will you get hurt? Yeah, most likely. Let's bring back all the extra, non-soulish dangers: STDs and AIDS and pregnancy. Those are very real things that really affect people. No one came up with that stuff to scare teenagers straight, you know. It all exists, and if you pretend it doesn't, you're at risk of chopping up your mouth with the steak knife.

Let's talk about pregnancy for a moment, as this is where I have, I'd like to think, a pretty good degree of expertise. I have four biological children (the other two are adopted). My first child was a complete surprise because, if I may be frank, my wife was on birth control *and* we were using condoms as a means of extra protection. Yet there my wife was, as pregnant as you can get.

> "I was in a serious relationship for a time with a boy I really shouldn't have been in a relationship with. We dated for eleven months, and he cheated on me the whole time. It broke my heart." —Kat, 17

Moving on to child #2: We'd decided that our first child needed a sibling, so we started trying. We got pregnant on, I'm not kidding, our first try.

Child #3 was another surprise, though we knew what we were getting into. We'd just gone through a rough patch in our marriage, but we'd emerged on the other side closer than ever. And we decided to celebrate closely, just once. And we figured, with God's sense of humor, that we'd get pregnant that one time, just like the last time, and we were right.

Child #4 was a very unexpected Christmas present that arose, again, from a single encounter.

We are, or at least should be, the poster family for abstinence. Because, honestly, I can speak from experience that it really does take only *one* time to get pregnant, no matter how much you think it won't happen. I can count on my fingers the number of times we've put ourselves in that situation, and we have four kids as a result.

Now, we've had our children in the context of a loving, committed marital relationship, and I wouldn't give back any of my children for anything. They are definitely a blessing, but they're a blessing that requires a lot of care and provision, and I'm thankful we had ours at a time in life when we're able to give them that.

"I think people expect too much out of high school relationships. I know people who were sure they were going to get married, and they gave each other promise rings and then three months later broke up. I would never do that." — Jenava, 17

Here's what I'm hoping you're taking away from this: Sex is a marvelous, miraculous, sacred thing. It is an act of worship, but it is worship in the holiest, most treasured way possible. It is nothing to be taken lightly, no matter what our culture says about it.

And it will still be there when you eventually get married.

WHAT ABOUT THE BIG "M"?

Here's a topic that I found was *never* addressed in my high school years. A topic for which I desperately wanted answers. A topic that couldn't be brought up without a bunch of under-the-breath snickering from most of my friends. A topic *so* taboo that even just the word is difficult to read.

Masturbation.

Yikes! It's tough to bring up, isn't it? It's something people love to joke about, but when it comes to dealing with it seriously, the information is quite limited. Is it a sin? Is it okay? What's the scoop?

Well, the Bible doesn't specifically ban masturbation, but we do find that "in sexual sin we violate the sacredness of our own bodies" (1 Corinthians 6:18). So is masturbation a violation of our bodies' sacredness?

Let me ask you this: When/if you masturbate, how much is going on mentally? Are you allowing your mind to go places it

shouldn't? Because, believe it or not, there is a (very)
small percentage of people in this world that can commit
self-sex and remain completely detached mentally and
emotionally. For them, it is a physical act that contains
nothing but biology.

Like I said, that percentage is excruciatingly small.

For the rest of humankind, masturbation is more than just
biology; it is a mental journey into forbidden areas, because your
mind and your attitude can betray you to sin. Simply *not* having
sex isn't enough to keep you pure. Jesus said so in Matthew
5:27-28: "You know the next commandment pretty well, too:
'Don't go to bed with another's spouse.' But don't think you've
preserved your virtue simply by staying out of bed. Your heart
can be corrupted by lust even quicker than your body. Those
leering looks you think nobody notices — they also corrupt."

Pretty powerful stuff. Obviously that passage was about adultery, which doesn't apply to you, but the principle is the same:
You can sin just by allowing your desires to flame out of control.

You aren't the only person to get tripped up in this area. I'd
say just about everyone who's ever existed has dealt with the issue
of masturbation at some time — or at many times — in their lives.
Granted, it's more a guy thing than a girl thing, though girls definitely struggle with it as well.

So how do you deal with it? Like every temptation to sin,
you take it to God. When you're faced with temptation — and
the Devil loves to tell you that failure is inevitable, so you might
as well just give in — you must counteract it with the truth of the
Bible. Personally, I love 1 Corinthians 10:13: "No test or temptation that comes your way is beyond the course of what others
have had to face. All you need to remember is that God will never
let you down; he'll never let you be pushed past your limit; he'll
always be there to help you come through it."

I JUST WANT TO BE UNDERSTOOD. HOW DO I COMMUNICATE WITH MY CLASSMATES SO THEY UNDERSTAND ME?

You're still trying to figure out who you are, for the most part. And part of that discovery process is figuring out ways to communicate well, how to communicate so you can be understood.

Again, this is where you have to realize, to some degree, that you can't do the understanding for them. You can't make your audience — your friends, your parents, your teachers, whomever — bend their minds to comprehend what you're trying to get across to them. It's up to you to bend your mind and communicate in a way they'll get.

I'm a writer for a living. It's my job to communicate with people so they can understand me. For example, I'm writing this book to you, a high school student. I wouldn't be doing my job well if I wrote the whole thing like this:

"When one wants to communicate on a strictly emotive plane, utilizing one's complete bevy of interpersonal skills, it is imperative that one regards one's audience with extreme impartiality and then proceeds accordingly."

That'd be fine if I wanted to write an instruction manual on communication for, say, engineers. You are not an engineer (at least not yet), so I'm trying to stick to more standard language that you find in your everyday life. I'm considering my audience and adjusting my brain to match up.

And the same thing should go for you. If you're having trouble communicating with someone, try to flip the whole scene over. Look at it from their point of view — from their life experience.

Let's look at this another way: Have you ever traveled in a foreign country? I went to Spain

on a missions trip the summer between my junior and
senior years, and while I loved the country, the language
barrier was a bit of a problem. My first morning there, I went
to a corner bakery to buy a croissant for breakfast (hey, I was in
Europe—I figured I needed to eat something European).

I pointed to the croissant I wanted and held up one finger
to indicate that I wanted one. The man behind the counter said
something in Spanish to me that I didn't comprehend. I widened
my eyes and shrugged my shoulders to let him know I was lost,
and you know what he did? He said the same exact thing, only
slower and louder.

This happens a lot in foreign countries. (We do it too, just
so you know.) Anyway, I had no idea what he was saying until he
held up his hand and rubbed his fingers against his thumb.

Ah. Money.

I plunked down some coins, and he took the appropriate ones.
"Gracias," I said.

The transaction was difficult because the man behind the
counter didn't speak my language and didn't really try, at first. It
wasn't until he went to pantomime that we were able to get things
done.

Later on that same missions trip, we hit up that delightfully
Spanish restaurant called McDonald's, if only for the kitsch of
eating fast food in a not-so-fast country. The menu was, of course,
in Spanish (it really did say "Grande Mac"!), and I fast determined
that I wanted some Chicken McNuggets, which, as I recall, were
listed as "McNuggets de Pantatres." I'm probably wrong on the exact
wording, but let's just go with it for the purposes of our story.

I got up to the counter and, determined to avoid the confu-
sion from my croissant episode, got out my money and prepared
to order in Spanish. The kid behind the counter just looked at me
when it was my turn.

"McNuggets de Pantatres," I said as confidently as I could, but sure I was mangling the language.

He gave me a puzzled look. "Eh?"

I cleared my throat and said, with decidedly less confidence, "Um, M-McNuggets . . . de Panta . . . tres?"

Clear as day, he replied, "You mean Chicken McNuggets?"

Ahem. "Um, yeah."

He spoke my language. He communicated with me, and everything worked out okay.

Want to be understood? Take a look at the way you're talking, through the other person's eyes.

HOW DO I DEAL WITH CONFRONTATION?

This is something that is hardly unique to the high school experience. You're going to have problems with people for the rest of your life — it's just part of the human experience. We're all different, and we're all stumbling into each other, and sooner or later, we're either going to get mad or make someone mad — or both.

But what do you do when that happens? What do you do when that one girl makes a catty comment in your direction? Or what about when things get heated during a pickup basketball game and that dude starts throwing elbows trying to pull down an offensive rebound?

What if *you're* the one making the catty comment or throwing the elbows and you suddenly feel bad about it? What should you do?

"There are certain conflicts I want to sweep under the rug and pretend didn't happen – bigger things that are just weird. But then there are other conflicts that I want to talk through with people because I want to be their friend still." – Haden, 16

It's all about forgiveness. That should be your key word. The concept of forgiveness is crucial to God, and it should be crucial to you.

Here's why. Just after He delivers the Lord's Prayer as a model for us to pray, Jesus unloads these words: "In prayer there is a connection between what God does and what you do. You can't get forgiveness from God, for instance, without also forgiving others. If you refuse to do your part, you cut yourself off from God's part" (Matthew 6:14-15).

You want forgiveness from God? (The correct answer is "Yes," by the way.) You have to forgive others. Even if they've hurt you, you have to forgive them. Don't hold in bitterness or anger or hatred, because that stuff will just drag you down. Let it go and let God deal with it for you.

So let's say you're all mad over something someone said or did to you. My recommendation would be to first calm down before you do anything. The worst thing is to confront someone while you're angry, because you're less in control of your tongue. Also, any amount of confrontation is going to put the other person on the defensive. If you come in with your guns blazing, it will put them on the defensive even more so. Besides, Proverbs 15:1 tells us, "A gentle response defuses anger, but a sharp tongue kindles a temper-fire."

Is it wrong to be angry? No. The Bible is plain that anger is an okay emotion to feel—you just have to use it correctly: "Go ahead and be angry. You do well to be angry — but don't use your anger as fuel for revenge. And don't stay angry. Don't go to bed angry. Don't give the Devil that kind of foothold in your life" (Ephesians 4:26-27).

In other words, don't let your anger use you. Keep it under control. Calm down. Here comes my favorite word: *perspective*. Get some. Realize that, in the grand scheme of things, this is not a big deal.

Now, I'm talking about your average, garden-variety confrontation here. I'm not talking about something extreme where maybe someone threatened your life or anything like that. Something like that happens? You need to consult the authorities, or at least someone in charge like a principal or a teacher you trust. But for minor things like disagreements, you have to retain perspective.

After you're calm, go to that person and try to work it out, just the two of you, if you can. Chances are, once the dust has settled and both of you have had time to calm down, you'll be able to find some understanding and resolve your differences. Most people are good-hearted enough to do that.

> "For some reason, lunch is a big deal at my school. We don't have cliques, really, because people float a lot, so cliques tend to be who you're sitting with at the moment. If you have a conflict, you just choose not to sit by that person at lunch. It's a horrible way to solve a conflict." — Josh, 16

But in the end, you have no control over whether they listen or not. You can only do your best to bring reconciliation, and you can find forgiveness in only your heart, not theirs. Their actions and reactions are their own; you can't control them. So don't try.

If they won't hear you, leave them to God and love them anyway.

HOW DO I LEARN TO TAKE CRITICISM? HOW DO I LEARN TO CRITICIZE OTHERS — CORRECTLY?

If you can figure this one out, you'll be miles ahead of most adults.

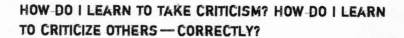

"Everyone has their breaking point. It depends on how far you want to go to please people. You can want everyone to think you're as good as them, but I think everybody gets to a point where they just want to be good enough that people don't confront them about it either way." — Tyler, 17

Criticism seems to come with the territory of teenage-dom, but it doesn't always have to. One of the many struggles you probably have is the feeling that you don't measure up to your peers. Come on, admit it. I was a student once; I know what it's like. There's just this constant nagging that you're missing the mark somehow.

I'll be honest with you: That doesn't go away when you hit adulthood. Oh, it may lessen, or get pushed out of the way occasionally, but in moments of clarity and silence, you can often feel it again, fighting its way to the surface.

Anyway, we often try to counteract this feeling of inadequacy by criticizing others. The idea is that if we feel low, instead of rising above others, we do what we can to make them even lower than us. It's the wrong way to get where we feel we need to be, but it's the easy way, so we take it.

However — and this is a big however — there are times in life when we'll need to either critique someone or be critiqued. This is different from outright criticism that's given out of spite or fear or any of the lesser emotions. I'm talking about legitimate critique.

An example: I was in the fall play during my senior year in high school. I played a coldhearted congressman who'd sent his slightly offbeat mother to an insane asylum packed with other offbeat people. Since I'd never *been* a coldhearted congressman before, let alone played one, I didn't really have a whole lot of experience to draw from. Sure, I had ideas, but I didn't know for sure if they were any good. Add to that the fact that I'd never been on stage before, and I think it'd be fair to say I was behind the curve.

Now, at that point, I had two options: I could either bully my way through the part, doing everything how I thought it should be done, or I could seek some critique from the director and listen to what she had to say.

But hearing — and using — critique in that sense meant I had to admit that I didn't know what I was doing. And let me tell you, that's a hard nut to give up, because I hate being wrong. Even worse, I hate admitting that I don't know something, especially when I'm supposed to know it.

And I'm going to be honest with you: It wasn't that easy hearing what my director had to say. Obviously I'd done something right initially — she'd cast me in the role, so something must've been there. But in order to take the character to the next level, where it needed to be, I had to submit to her critique.

Now, she did it as best she could, the way a good director

should do it—she wasn't belittling or any of that nonsense that happens a lot. And the thing I had to keep in mind was this: We were all working toward the same goal. She wasn't giving me direction to make herself feel superior or to make me feel stupid—we were both hoping to make the character, and therefore the play, better.

This is the way critique works. Very rarely do people in authority over you—teachers, parents, principals, youth pastors —tell you what to do because they're on a power trip. (That stuff gets saved for later in life when you start to work in the business world.) They critique you because they want you to grow as a person—because they see potential that needs to be guided. And the only way to guide that potential is through critique. Just keep in mind that they aren't attacking you, and they aren't dragging you down as a person. They aren't out to destroy you. They're just trying to help.

And the same should go when the shoe's on the other foot. Are you being critical of others? Are you doing it because you're trying to help them become better people, or are you doing it just to make yourself feel better, for whatever reason? Where's your heart? What's your motivation? Why are you doing it?

HOW DO I HANG OUT WITH OTHER PEOPLE AND AVOID GETTING THEIR BAD HABITS?

When I was a kid, I think in sixth, seventh grade, I went to band camp.

Yes, sound the nerd alert. I was in band, like all cool people.

So I was at band camp with my friend Corby, spending an entire week at the University of Arkansas to learn how to play my instrument (cornet, which is like a trumpet but different, if you must know) better. I was away from my family and in a "secular" environment for the first time in my life, and I'm sure my parents were mortified.

Anyway, Corby and I started hanging out with this older kid named Steve, a sax player who wore a gold link chain around his neck with a matching bracelet. He also had slicked-back hair and wore loud Hawaiian shirts. He was a grade ahead of us, and he let us hang out with him the whole week. He was *so* cool, man.

Steve had this odd way of speaking, where he kept his mouth mostly closed, but he didn't mumble his words — he whined them. It's like the dialogue he spoke was air being forced out of a balloon when you stretch the balloon's opening out to make it squeak and squeal. And he said everything like a question.

So cool.

When I got home from band camp, I was talking to my mother in the kitchen while she made dinner, and she asked, "Why are you talking like that?"

"Like what?" I said.

"Whining like that. When did you start that?"

I didn't even realize it, but I'd begun talking like Steve, God help me. I guess I just looked up to him so much while at band camp that I had adopted his speech without knowing I'd done it.

Mom then gave me her full opinion on that particular style of speaking:

"Stop it."

And that was that. Problem solved. I went back to my normal voice with no difficulty and have never unintentionally spoken that way since.

But it's hard, isn't it? To remain true to yourself when presented with the characteristics of someone else, someone you — maybe even subconsciously — want to impress. And it's doubly hard when you realize you don't even *really* know everything about yourself yet—that's part of what you're trying to figure out in this time of your life.

What can you do? Take it to God. In Romans 12:1-2, the Bible says, "Take your everyday, ordinary life—your sleeping, eating, going-to-work, and walking-around life—and place it before God as an offering. Embracing what God does for you is the best thing you can do for him. Don't become so well-adjusted to your culture that you fit into it without even thinking. Instead, fix your attention on God. You'll be changed from the inside out. Readily recognize what he wants from you, and quickly respond to it. Unlike the culture around you, always dragging you down to its level of immaturity, God brings the best out of you, develops well-formed maturity in you."

> "It's that time in our lives where we're supposed to be learning who we are. We aren't supposed to already know. We're supposed to know what we like, we're supposed to have opinions, but we aren't supposed to know exactly who we are just yet. We're still learning." — Kaitlin, 17

You avoid changing yourself to match up with other people by letting God change you first. From the inside out. By taking your entire life to Him and welcoming Him into it and saying, "All right, God—do whatever's necessary."

It's a tough thing to do, and it doesn't stop when you get out of high school. There are always going to be things you have to give up to Him, ways you're going to need transformation.

Instead of getting other people's bad habits, crack open the Bible and try to get some of God's good ones. I sincerely hope this survival guide isn't the only book you're reading right now — I hope you're also taking time in your life to check out God's Word to see what else He has to say on these topics. Because it's there where God can speak to you, where He can help you develop the good habits you need to become an influence on your world.

HOW DO I DEAL WITH PEOPLE WHO ARE DIFFERENT FROM ME?

When you look at the world around you, it's easy to spot the differences. Those kids are goths, those kids are preps, and those kids are jocks. Those kids are African-American, those kids are Asian, and those kids are Hispanic. Those kids are straight; those kids are gay.

In some respects, *everyone* is different from you. Your siblings may have the same parents as you, but no one was born under the same conditions as you: the exact same genetic parents, on the exact same day, at the exact same time. Even identical twins are born minutes apart.

> "We're used to thinking of discrimination as white people versus black people, and it's not just like that anymore. It's everybody versus everybody."
> —Kaitlin, 17

Each little experience you have is another part of the recipe that makes up the big pot of stew called "your life." And because no one has had the *exact* same experiences as you, no one is *exactly* like you. It's the same for all of us. So in order to bond with others, we tend to divide ourselves along lines of similarity: people of the same background, people who like the same style of music, people who have the same faith, and so on.

> "It's almost like you take the cliques out of high school and expand it, and that's the way the world is now. It's every person versus every other person."
> — Jennifer, 17

But what do you do when you're plunked down in the middle of one of those groups you don't know anything about? What do you do when you cross those lines of similarity into foreign territory? What do you do when someone else crosses those lines into your territory?

Let's look at what Jesus did. In John 4:1-30, Jesus had an encounter with a woman from Samaria, a woman who was in such a bad state of shame that she got water from the town well in the middle of the day, when the sun was hottest, because she knew no one would be there. She wanted to avoid people; she didn't want anyone to see her.

But she ran into Jesus at this well, and He read her mail. He knew everything about her. And He was a *Jew*. Jews and Samaritans didn't get along well — at the time, the Jews viewed Samaritans as something like second-class citizens. So it probably blew this woman's mind that this all-knowing Jew would even talk to her.

It certainly blew the disciples' minds. We see that in verse 27, which comes right after Jesus tells this woman that He's the long-awaited Messiah: "Just then his disciples came back. They were shocked. They couldn't believe he was talking with that kind of a woman. No one said what they were all thinking, but their faces showed it."

But Jesus talked to her, and it changed her life. She originally wanted to steer clear of everyone, but you know what she did after her one conversation with Jesus? She went back into the village and told everyone what had happened to her and that they all needed to come meet Him.

We see this same thing again in the parable Jesus tells about the Good Samaritan in Luke 10:30-35. You know the story: A guy's walking down the road when he gets attacked and beaten up by robbers, then is left for dead. A priest happens along and doesn't help; a Levite (who, incidentally, would be of the priestly lineage of the Jews) does the same thing: crosses to the other side of the road to avoid the man. Then a dirty ol' Samaritan, ick, comes along, takes care of the guy, puts him up in the inn, and pays for his restoration.

And then Jesus brings it home, as we see in the following exchange from verses 36-37: [Jesus asked,] "What do you think? Which of the three became a neighbor to the man attacked by robbers?"

"The one who treated him kindly," the religion scholar responded.

Jesus said, "Go and do the same."

Boom. Jesus just told a Jew — and a scholarly, religious Jew, at that — to be like a *Samaritan*. That was *huge*. Because the essence of Jesus' statement, and His exchange with the Samaritan woman, was this: Look at people as people. It doesn't matter who they are or what clique or social group they affiliate themselves with. If they're doing good, that's good. If they're doing bad — even if they're in your same group (like those two "priestly" Jews who passed up the hurt man) — that's bad.

Jesus wants us to break it down to character. He wants us to dig deeper in our lives, to get down to the heart of the matter and find a way to relate with others so that we can relate *Him* to them. It doesn't matter how different or similar they are — they're His creation, and He loves them, and He wants you to love them too.

CHAPTER 4

YOU AND SCHOOL

Who could ever have told God what to do or taught him his business? What expert would he have gone to for advice, what school would he attend to learn justice? What god do you suppose might have taught him what he knows, showed him how things work? (Isaiah 40:13-14)

I said to myself, "I know more and I'm wiser than anyone before me in Jerusalem. I've stockpiled wisdom and knowledge." What I've finally concluded is that so-called wisdom and knowledge are mindless and witless — nothing but spitting into the wind. Much learning earns you much trouble. The more you know, the more you hurt. (Ecclesiastes 1:16-18)

Wise men and women are always learning, always listening for fresh insights. (Proverbs 18:15)

WHAT ABOUT CHEATING? I MEAN, I KNOW IT'S WRONG, BUT COME ON—CAN'T IT BE OKAY SOMETIMES?

Boy, is this temptation *always* with you. "How so?" you might ask, thinking that you're never really going to take tests after high school. Ah, but you *are*. No, you don't take final exams or anything of that nature, necessarily, but you do encounter quite a few tests—almost on a daily basis, if you think about it.

You encounter these tests now, actually. You've encountered them your whole life.

You know what I'm talking about: those little tests of character, when temptation strikes. It always happens when no one's looking (someone—I forget who—once said, "Character is who you are when no one else is around"), when you're all by yourself and you get the hankering (I'm from Oklahoma, which makes it okay for me to use that word) to do something a little askew. Maybe watch some TV or a movie you know you shouldn't. Hit up the internet for some destinations that would require a little covering of your tracks.

Cheating speaks to a larger issue of integrity, and the main question you have to consider when talking about this type of thing is this: Are you trying to get away with something?

I have a hypothetical situation for you. Well, it's not that hypothetical, in that I had it happen to me all the time when I was in high school. I'll admit it: I was smart back then. Not street-smart, mind you. Book smart. Test smart. I was in all those fancy math classes like trigonometry and calculus (which, by the way, I don't remember a thing about—I just took them because it was expected of me).

Anyway, trig was a nightmare. We had tons of homework every day, which required *a lot* of busywork. You know, that standard math homework motif where you have to do all the even-numbered problems, because the answers to the odd-numbered problems are in the back? And there are, like, forty problems? Plus, this was complicated stuff that required graphing calculators where you had to use all those buttons with the funky symbols. You could generally fit about two problems on a piece of paper, college-ruled.

So just about everyone in my trig class gathered at a local pizza restaurant every day after school. We pitched in to get a large pepperoni and then "worked together" on that day's homework assignment. Now, the idea was for each of us to do our own work, then compare answers or methods to discover the exact way to work each problem. If several of us got the same answer, we could all be fairly certain we'd done the work correctly.

Of course, there was a *vast* temptation to coast — to let everyone else do the work and just copy down their answers. Would that be wrong? (Correct answer: "Of course.")

But what if I did one problem, checked it against everyone else's work, and found that my answer was different? Would it have been wrong for me to just list their answer instead of mine? After all, I'd done the work, right? And wasn't that the whole point of the homework assignment? To do the work? So what if my work didn't line up with my answer — the teacher was never going to check my work; she'd never know.

And this is where the areas get gray and the slope becomes slippery, because you're going to be put into situations like that from now 'til you die. Situations where you start to ask yourself rationalizing questions, desperately attempting to reason your way into doing something that could possibly maybe might be potentially wrong. Not even "wrong" in the strictest sense of the word — just "less right."

The giant waving red flag in the middle of all those

questions consists of a mere three words (four, if you remove the apostrophe): "They'll never know."

That is the phrase every human being tells themselves when they're about to try to get away with something. The second it enters your head, run the other direction. Just hearing those words with your mental ears is enough to let you know it's the wrong thing.

But what about situations where you're with other people? That dreaded "peer pressure" everyone's so fond of talking about? This is just as much a cheating danger as cheating all by yourself, often compounded by that "Come on, everyone else is doing it" mentality I'm sure you're already familiar with. Yes, it's overworn and cliché, but it still exists.

So in my own school example, the peer pressure thing was a *big* temptation factor. Many of my fellow students did exactly what I described: They split up the problems, each worked one or two, and then copied everyone else's work. Then they'd finish their pizza and go hang out, leaving a few of us who were determined to do the work the right way.

And the galling thing? Those kids were *never* found out. They never got in trouble, never got expelled or had their grade lowered an entire letter. They got away with it—and it was so frustrating.

But you know what I realized back then, that you would do well to realize right now? I wasn't in charge of those guys. I couldn't do anything about the way they were living their lives, if they really wanted to do that. All I could do anything about was me. I could make sure *I* was doing the right thing.

God's pretty clear about this in the Bible, right there in the book of Romans. Check this out: "Don't hit back; discover beauty in everyone. If you've got it in you, get along with everybody. Don't insist on getting even; that's not for you to do. 'I'll do the judging,' says God. 'I'll take care of it'" (12:17-19).

The point is, you need to take care of you. The Bible puts it this way: "Make a careful exploration of who you are and the work you have been given, and then sink yourself into that. Don't be impressed with yourself. Don't compare yourself with others. Each of you must take responsibility for doing the creative best you can with your own life" (Galatians 6:4-5).

God will always smile on integrity. Always. Whether you're ever recognized for it by your friends, or your teachers, or the National Honor Society, or anyone else, God will recognize it, and He'll smile on it.

The same thing goes for stuff that doesn't feel like out-and-out cheating. Like plagiarism. It's *so* easy (and tempting) to copy and paste your research paper from Wikipedia into a Word document, but it's going to backfire in many ways. For one thing, you never know how many of your fellow students are going to do something so boneheaded. For another thing, information isn't necessarily true just because you found it online.

The internet—yes, even that bastion of truth Wikipedia—is packed with misconceptions, falsehoods, half-truths, errors, and flat-out lies. Unless you're getting information from reliable sources (and no, your friend's cousin's half sister's friend who's in community college's MySpace page doesn't count), you run the risk of getting nothing but regurgitated nonsense.

You know the way the internet works: One person throws something inaccurate up there, maybe just to be dumb, or maybe just because they're expressing an opinion. Someone else reads it and copies/pastes it onto their own page. Now it's wrong on *two* places on the internet. Multiply *ad infinitum* until myth becomes legend and legend becomes fact.

Not that the internet is all bad. There are tons of valid sites out there, and it's super-handy for research. I used it to research this book, for example. I use it all the time, especially to find handy Bible quotes to share with you, my dear reader.

You just have to be careful where you find your information. And when you *do* find info you can trust, you have to be careful what you do with it. You can't just copy and paste it from your browser into your word processing software (this is where I could insert a joke about also needing to format it properly, adjusting the font and point size, but you already know that one).

The whole point of your paper is that you seek out information and then show your teacher/professor that you found it, processed it, and understood it well enough to write it down—coherently and in your own words.

This is another thing you'll need to learn for your adult life: writing. I hate to break it to you, but it's just the way things are. Especially with how many keyboards are in use in the world, and how many more are projected to be in use as technology evolves. And the shorthand you use for sending instant and text messages isn't going to cut it. That's fine between friends, but you aren't always going to be writing to friends in the adult world.

Even in the outskirts of the business world, you will be forced to display moderate writing skill, usually in the form of email. And no, business writing and academic writing aren't the same thing, but if you get plenty of practice in school, you'll at least have the basics of punctuation, capitalization, and spelling down. Plus, you'll spend all that practice time figuring out how to communicate your thoughts accurately and clearly through the written word—that's where it all really pays off.

I'm not saying you have to become the next Shakespeare (or J. K. Rowling, for that matter); you just need to be able to get your point across. And as pointless as they often seem, research papers and other assignments like them help you get there. Just don't go stealing other people's work and passing it off as your own. You know better.

ARE DUE DATES ALL THAT IMPORTANT?

My publisher will probably tell you that I'm the wrong person to answer this question, as I consistently turn my books in a week after they're due. I tell you this not to make you think it's okay to be late on your assignments; I tell you so you'll understand that due dates are never going to leave you. Also, I want you to see the link between your school experience and the experience of the "real" world. You have trouble turning stuff in on time? So do I.

We should be friends.

Actually, this is a pretty easy one to handle, if you have a little self-discipline. Now, granted, you're going to have the occasional hard-nosed teacher who gives you impossible due dates for projects just to see what you'll do. Occasionally, you'll have teachers who seem to have forgotten that you have other classes besides theirs, and the teachers of those other classes are also demanding some of your time.

So what do you do in these situations? Well, first of all, don't panic. Panicking isn't going to get you anywhere. In the words of Jesus, "Give your entire attention to what God is doing right now, and don't get worked up about what may or may not happen tomorrow. God will help you deal with whatever hard things come up when the time comes" (Matthew 6:34).

If you feel the urge to panic about a due date, just stop, take a deep breath, and say a prayer for wisdom. This is probably not the first due date you've ever faced, and it certainly won't be the last. Me? I try to maintain perspective about them. While they are important, my deadlines are not necessarily aptly named—if I miss one, I won't *die*. Neither will anyone in my family. We won't all go hungry. Lightning won't strike the antenna of my Pathfinder. A meteorite will not come crashing into my living room and emit a mysterious odor that causes us all to grow gills.

What *will* happen? A date on the calendar will pass. And in the grand scheme of things, that isn't so bad.

Okay, okay, okay; please get this: *I'm not telling you to blow off your schoolwork.* Hear that. Loud and clear. Please. I'm just offering the panic-prone some perspective.

Now, what else happens if I turn in my books late? I force other people to rearrange their schedules and work harder to pick up my slack. If I'm too late, I might void the contract I signed, which means I wouldn't get paid. If I'm late all the time, I'd get a reputation for being late, which would turn off publishers in general and convince them not to hire me as a writer, making it tougher for me to get work. See? A bad habit can turn into a career obstacle pretty quickly.

Fortunately, that hasn't happened.

Which, again, is why you have a great opportunity to learn now how to turn stuff in on time.

HOW THE HECK AM I SUPPOSED TO FOCUS LONG ENOUGH TO GET ALL THIS STUFF TURNED IN ON TIME?

The key is to manage your workload. This is a key for me, and it's a key for you. Look at what you have to get done and set priorities. Don't try to tackle the whole mountain at once, either. Do one thing at a time. And reward yourself for getting pieces done.

If you have to, set the timer on your mobile phone for ten minutes and see how much you can get done in that time. Gradually increase your time until you can work all the way through an assignment. (By the way, don't go overboard with the rewards. If you last ten minutes, you haven't earned a whole movie or evening with friends.)

Find a place where you always work. For example, I am typing these very words while sitting in a Starbucks near my house. Why? Because I'm a big movie fan, and I'm having trouble keeping myself off the internet to read about upcoming releases. Also, I desperately want to check a few sports scores and use the internet to keep up with some games that are being played tonight.

What does that have to do with Starbucks? They don't offer free internet access, and I don't want to pay their monthly fee for Wi-Fi, so I'm currently rolling without any internet. No internet to divert my attention means I can focus on writing my book without distraction.

Also, being away from home helps me focus. Let's say I unplugged the wireless router at my house as an internet deterrent. That's fine, but my couch is right by the kitchen — it's way too easy for me to decide to "take a break" and have a bowl of cereal. Or ice cream. And then check to see what's on TV. Oh! There's that *Simpsons* episode I love. Lemme check that out. Oh yeah, *Lost* is on tonight and it's just getting good. Boy, I'm hungry again — think I'll go grab some Taco Bell.

Argh! Sadly, this happens to me more than I care to admit. But for some reason, being in Starbucks helps me focus.

"The biggest problem at my school is time-wasting. All over, people are wasting their time, not even basing things on real things or real relationships. They just talk about things like movies or what's on TV. Ten years from now, are you really going to remember that television show you watched? Are you going to look back and say, 'Ha ha, that one episode was really funny'?" — Haden, 16

What helps you focus? We've already talked a little bit about this, as far as your learning environment goes, but an important part about that is making sure you're free of distractions—which means you have to identify your distractions. For my wife, TV isn't a distraction, but her cell phone sure is. I could care less about talking on the phone—I kinda hate doing it, honestly (not with her, by the way—she's the one exception). My wife can talk to anyone on the phone, and talk for a long time. So if she's trying to focus on getting something done, her phone is the first thing to go.

What's your distraction? Maybe you have more than one. Figure it (them) out, and then have the courage to chuck them aside (just temporarily, remember) in pursuit of the bigger goal of meeting your due date. Recruit your friends to help keep you honest, if you must. Hand off your cell phone or cable modem to someone if you need to. Have your friends check up on you, and vice versa. You know what you need to do—do it.

HOMEWORK SUCKS. DO I HAVE TO DO IT?

Good question. Homework is one of those things
you sort of have to live with. It is *always* going to be
connected to school, no matter how much you hate
it or want to get around it, so it's best just to accept the fact that
you *will* have to do homework.

> "I don't like homework — that's kind of obvious — but
> I do understand that it's teaching me. Like, if you
> repeat stuff to yourself, it helps you memorize it. So I
> understand its value, but it's tough to balance every-
> thing with school and a job and all that." — Grant, 17

Of course, though much homework seems completely pointless and repetitive, there's a reason for it, despite any claims you
may make to the contrary. The whole point, whether you agree
with it or not, is to give you plenty of practice at whatever particular thing you're supposed to be learning, from graphing func-
tions to diagramming sentences (a practice that you will *never* use
in the real world but that really does come in handy for identify-
ing the parts of speech) to researching the presidential decrees
of Rutherford B. Hayes. The more you practice something, the
more likely you are to remember it when you need to.

Now, as a functioning adult, I'm going to level with you:
Most of the knowledge you learn in school isn't really all that
important. Honestly, I remember a handful of facts from my high
school years (which weren't that long ago). Although I'm often
surprised while watching *Jeopardy!* or some such quiz-type show
how many of those meaningless facts are still rattling around in
my brain.

Does that mean homework isn't important and that you should blow it off?

Absolutely not.

Because while you may not take the information from your homework into your adult life, you *will* take the practice of perseverance. In the big picture, that is the point of homework after all. You are in school training to be an adult. That's why you're there. Well, part of being an adult is having a solid education, knowledge-wise, but an even larger part of being an adult is having solid habits and practices.

Think of school as training for your career. Now, you don't always have to think of it that way—I don't want to ruin the fun parts of it—but it doesn't hurt to imagine your life outside the 8:00-2:30 grind of education. I know it seems far away, but there will come a time when you leave the school grounds and are expected to contribute to our society and, you know, get a job. Not the part-time kind, either—an honest-to-goodness, for-real job where you earn enough money to eat and find shelter and, should you so desire, raise a family.

And all those things require a very nasty word: discipline. Ick. I don't like it either. I don't like deadlines and taxes and responsibility and doing stuff I don't enjoy just because it's my job—but I do them because that's part of the gig. It's right there in the Bible, right up front. Because of the sin he let into this world, Adam is informed, by God Himself, no less, "You'll get your food the hard way, Planting and tilling and harvesting, sweating in the fields from dawn to dusk, Until you return to that ground yourself, dead and buried; you started out as dirt, you'll end up as dirt" (Genesis 3:18-19).

Yay! Isn't that *awesome?* Life is just going to be one meaningless chore! You'll perform super-difficult tasks just to sustain yourself, and then after all that, you'll die! Now, who's ready to *work*?

Fortunately for most of us, we don't grow food anymore; instead we get jobs to pay for the food we can't or won't grow. And the housing we tend not to build for ourselves. And the clothes we generally don't stitch together on our own. There aren't many homespun shoe cobblers out there anymore (although, if you think about it, how hard could it be to make a decent pair of flip-flops?).

So we work. And unless our name is Bill Gates (or Steve Jobs for you Mac users), we're probably going to have to work hard. We may not toil in a crop field under a hot sun, but we all toil at some point in our lives.

And that's where your homework comes in. Think of it as practice toil. It's mini-toil. Toil with fewer consequences than adult-life toil. If you screw up this toil, you aren't necessarily putting your entire life in jeopardy. A couple of bad grades on research papers won't end in getting the electricity shut off (of course, a single missed bill won't either—you have to miss a couple in a row). Continued bad grades will result in some consequences, of course, but at least those consequences won't happen in the dark.

In the end, your homework assignments are a perfect way for you to try on adult living. You get the chance to see how it fits, check yourself out in the mirror, and make any adjustments necessary before the stakes get any higher.

SO HOW DO I GET BETTER AT HOMEWORK THEN?

"Homework shouldn't be called homework because I always do it in first hour."—Phil, 14

Ah, but how to make those adjustments? There are a few rules of thumb when it comes to homework. For starters, don't make the mistake of assuming that everyone learns the same way. Some people learn best by hearing, some people by reading, and others by doing. Most of us are a combination of the three but have a tendency to prefer one or the other.

I'm a reader. I can read directions like crazy and completely understand them. My wife? Forget it. She learns by doing. She could read directions to something, then go to work on it and be completely lost. But show her how to do it and she'll have it in seconds.

Figure out your strengths and play to them. If you learn by doing, don't try to get by with some light reading. Determine a way to *do* what you're learning. If it's math, that's a cinch—just work whatever problems have been assigned. If it's more of a fact-oriented subject like English or history, write down whatever facts you need to know. Write them more than once if you have to. The act of writing sends the information through your system, if that makes sense, from your eyes to your brain to your hands to the paper and then back up to your eyes.

If you learn by reading, you probably hate math with everything in you. Most of your other subjects are cake, but math? That's just a whole lot of doing. So try this out: Study those dreaded word problems. See how the concepts relate to each other. Look for the relationships between the word problems and the straight-up homework problems; see how one fits together with the other.

Are you a hearing-style learner? There's no law that says you can't learn by hearing your own voice. I have elements of hearing in my learning, and I frequently talked myself through math problems, if only as a way of reinforcing what I'd read. If reading doesn't get any facts into your head, try reading those facts aloud—in the privacy of your bedroom, of course. We don't want people to think you're a weirdo.

Another key to getting your homework done is the environment you're doing it in. Some people (like me) thrive while working in noisy areas. I wrote this book almost exclusively in coffee shops and other high-traffic, high-noise areas—usually with headphones on and my iTunes cranked. If I'm not hearing the whir of the milk steamer filtered through some Switchfoot or *Lord of the Rings* movie scores while I write, something just isn't right. If I'm at home, I keep the headphones going and usually have the TV on. (One type of noise not conducive to writing? My children, mainly because their noise consists of tugging on me and asking to play video games on my computer.)

Now that you've read this, some of you think I'm crazy. You're like a former coworker of mine who had to have absolute silence while he worked—not exactly the best trait for a cubicle area that saw quite a bit of foot traffic in the building. Maybe you're the same way. If so, don't try to do your homework with your iPod hanging out of your ears at the bus station. Get someplace quiet so you can concentrate.

Experiment with environments. If it's a nice day, drag your schoolwork outside to a park bench or picnic table. You may do great at a desk in your room, or you may prefer to lounge on your bed while you crank out that day's assignments. Try working on stuff with friends at a nearby coffee shop (be sure to buy something before you camp out there for the evening, though—they don't take kindly to squatters). Sooner or later, you'll figure out what works best for you.

You may be thinking, *But, Adam, I'm not always going to have the luxury of changing my environment in the real world. Shouldn't I practice now by forcing myself to work in an environment that might not be the best?* And if you're thinking that, you're very astute. Good job.

However, in the real world, if you *could* change your environment, you would, assuming you would need to change. Not everyone gets to choose their work environment, so at this stage of your life, take what you can get, while you can get it.

The main thing to keep in mind is the end goal of all that homework: to get a jump start on your future.

I HAVE THE FOCUS THING DOWN, BUT THIS STILL SEEMS LIKE SO MUCH WORK TO GET DONE. ANY IDEAS?

Okay, now that you've minimized your distractions, the next big step is actually a freeing one: Break your assignment into manageable chunks. For me, I know I'm not going to sit down and write a book in one sitting. If you have a big project, remember that you don't have to do it all at once.

Look at it this way: If your assignment was to eat a pizza in an hour, would you ball the whole thing up, cram it into your mouth as best you could, and try to have it choked down in ten minutes? Only if you waited until you had ten minutes left on the clock.

Give yourself plenty of time, and work on your assignment in bits and pieces. For instance, I'm taking this book a question at a time. I try to sit down and write one question answer at every sitting. This way, I'm not maxing out my brain capacity (not to mention my typing fingers and the chair resistance of my rear end) with big, long fifteen-hour stints behind the keyboard. Sure, I might get the work done that way, but I'll burn myself out, and I sure won't be helping you by working half-steam.

Make a plan. Don't be afraid to bust out the calendar and figure out a schedule for your schoolwork. If you have a research paper due in a week, don't wait six days to get cracking on it. Head to the library on day one. Process all that information on day two. Spend days three and four writing your paper. Edit it on day five (never turn in your rough draft—it isn't as good as you think it is while you're writing it). Take day six to put on the finishing touches and to write your bibliography. Turn it in the next day. Boom. Done. You finished your paper little by little, without stress and without feeling like you lost a ton of time doing it.

Prioritize. Do the most important, most time-critical work first. If you have an assignment that's due in three days and one that's due tomorrow and you have time to work on only one, which one should you do? Seems like a no-brainer, but you'd be surprised how many people don't think things through.

What else?

Make sure you understand the limitations your teacher has placed on the assignment. Is it something you're supposed to be doing solo, or can you enlist the help of your friends or family? One time for physics class, we had an "egg drop" contest. Each student had to construct a device that could protect an egg when it was dropped from the top of the school building. I went home and immediately sought help from my very-smart parents, who suggested the secret ingredient that led to my successful completion of the assignment: corn starch. I used it to insulate the egg and everything worked out great.

I guess the whole thing I'm getting at here is that you need to take advantage of every resource available to you, even the less obvious ones. Don't throw in the towel and start wringing your hands at the first signs of difficulty, even if an assignment seems impossible to figure out. Your teacher wouldn't assign it to you if it were impossible, but if you *did* get an impossible assignment, then it'll be impossible for everyone in the class and you'll all have a good laugh about it the next time you meet.

Just stay calm, relax, and keep chipping away until the job is done. You might surprise yourself at how satisfying it feels.

IS IT WRONG TO WANT TO BE POPULAR? HOW DO I GET INTO THE "IN" CROWD? HOW DO I GET OUT OF IT?

"When I was in junior high, I really wanted to be popular. Then last year, I just decided it didn't really matter. And when I made that decision to let it go, I started making more friends — real friends."
—Gabrielle, 16

American Idol has never been a singing competition, no matter how many times Simon Cowell says that it is. The show is nothing more than the world's biggest popularity contest, only with singing as a backdrop and a means of qualifying our opinions. If it *was* a singing competition, it would be on the radio. We decide how much we like (or dislike) contestants based on how they look, how they seem in real life, and how they interact with their fellow contestants.

American Idol is like the high school experience played out on a national stage. Doesn't it sometimes feel as if you're on the verge of getting voted out? Of going home? Don't you sometimes feel like looking into the camera and flashing your phone number with your fingers to try to get your classmates to vote for you?

Like it or not, popularity is a major part

of high school. There will always be students who draw more of a crowd than most, through looks or athleticism or outward fashion or just sheer charisma. Maybe you're one of those people. Or maybe you look at them and secretly want to be one of them. Or maybe you look at them and are glad you *aren't* them because you just want to do your own thing.

Whatever your feelings on popularity, you need to check your heart and your perspective on the issue. Are you looking to popularity to validate your own self-worth? Are you hoping to find love through the adoration of others? Are you just looking for a friend?

Validation and love and friendship are good things, and they're things we need and want. But we have to make sure our methods of obtaining them line up with God's Word — we shouldn't seek popularity just for the sake of being popular. We shouldn't strive for popularity in order to fill a void that God is meant to fill.

"If you're popular, you're popular. I don't think you should look at a person and say, 'Oh, that person's popular, so I'm going to try to be like them.' I'm not exactly 'popular,' and I don't want to try to be popular. If I get that way, it's fine, but I'd almost rather it not happen." — Jaime, 15

Let's turn to the Bible to see what it has to say. For example, Luke 6:26 addresses the issue directly: "There's trouble ahead when you live only for the approval of others, saying what flatters them, doing what indulges them. Popularity contests are not truth contests. . . . Your task is to be true, not popular."

This is Jesus talking here, and those are pretty strong words.

When it comes to popularity, there is a temptation to say, "Whatever it takes," and those words tend to come easily, especially the more we practice them. But Jesus directly said that kind of living will only bring trouble, because no matter how popular you get, no matter how many people approve of you, you'll never be able to maintain your popularity. Eventually, someone will stop esteeming you as highly, and then you'll be left with nothing but empty words.

But the truth? The truth is the opposite of empty. Sometimes it hurts, but it always fulfills. That's why Jesus said, "Your task is to be true, not popular."

What about Paul, the apostle? He was a popular guy—what did he think about it? We find the answer in Galatians 1:10: "Do you think I speak this strongly in order to manipulate crowds? Or curry favor with God? Or get popular applause? If my goal was popularity, I wouldn't bother being Christ's slave."

Ouch! Paul had a real way of bringing the issue home, didn't he? He was basically saying, "Look, I know I'm popular, but I could care less." Which probably only made him more popular because he didn't look desperate and needy about it.

But there is that longing within us that says we have to draw on the opinions of others to feel good about ourselves. I know this for a fact—every time I write a book, no matter how good I feel about it, when I send it off to the editor for the first time, I'm ultra-worried that they're going to come back and say it's crap. Because in my mind, if they do, that's a bunch of time wasted, and I must be a worthless writer, and I'm good for nothing, and blah blah blah.

> "In my school, everyone just kind of knows every-
> one, so no one's popular. If you're just friendly and
> outgoing, you're good." — Alex, 17

I'm sure your experiences are the same. We tend to crave the praise of others, and don't get me wrong — praise is a good thing. I make sure to praise my children all the time. If they do something even remotely right, I'm there with a high five and a "Good job" because I know that feeds their souls.

But we need to get those praises for the right reasons. We shouldn't crave approval as a substitute for love. Paul brought this up in 1 Corinthians 4:3: "It matters very little to me what you think of me, even less where I rank in popular opinion. I don't even rank myself. Comparisons in these matters are pointless." He knows he's valuable to God, and that's the only opinion that matters to him. It's why he called himself a "slave to Christ," as we saw a few paragraphs back.

So what about you? What are you looking for? Love? Acceptance? Encouragement? Turn to the truth. Look to God. Let Him show it to you.

> "The new way to fit in is to not fit in." — Tyler, 17

SHOULD I HAVE ANY EXTRACURRICULAR ACTIVITIES? ARE THEY WORTH ANYTHING AT ALL?

I think extracurricular activities are one of the best things about high school, mainly because there are just so many of them. Chances are, if you have any sort of interest in anything that isn't sleeping or video games, you'll be able to find something that grabs your attention, regardless of where you live.

"I find that extracurricular activities really helped me. My freshman year, I had competitive speech and soccer. Little things in my life got me stressed out, and soccer was one thing I could always go to, where I could just play and forget everything that was going on. I created many different friendships in soccer that allowed me to get through stuff, and I still have some of those friendships today." — Michael, 17

I graduated from a small high school of less than a thousand students, and we had about a kajillion extra things to do. Drama, band, athletics, language clubs, FFA, 4-H, FCA—I'm sure you can fill out the rest of this list.

But what's the point? Why participate? For starters, colleges like to see that you have interests outside academics. We all know many universities offer athletic scholarships, but you can also often get scholarships for other reasons, often tied to nonathletic extracurricular activities.

Colleges like students who are team players because everyone who comes onto their campus will reflect that campus in some way. They want to see students with broad horizons, with outside interests that will then broaden their student body. It's never a bad idea to participate in something that will broaden your horizons.

"I used to go to a really small school where there weren't a lot of opportunities for extracurricular opportunities other than the normal sports, and kids were really bad. They didn't have drive, they didn't have ambition. I saw so many more drug problems there than where I am now, at a larger school. Here kids have something to do, they have someplace to meet, to do something they like, with people they enjoy being around." — Kaitlin, 17

But aside from that, electives give you a chance to interact with people you may not ordinarily interact with. You're hanging out with people who are into the same stuff as you, so you're already well down the road of potential friendship. If you're into, say, Academic Bowl like I was (no snickers from the audience, please), then you're going to make friends with other people who like to hoard trivia in their head, then pretend they're on *Jeopardy!* and try to buzz in with a correct answer to win something for the school that no one will ever talk about.

Ahem.

The only big drawback with extracurricular activities is that having too many of them can take over your life. During my senior year, I was determined to have more clubs listed after my name in the yearbook than anyone else, so I pretty much joined everything I was eligible for. The result: I was spread too thin and couldn't afford as much time on my schoolwork as I maybe needed. I had to cut back a little just to reclaim my life. I didn't cut out all my activities, but I did give Academic Bowl a rest.

> "I enjoy theater. It's a way to escape, a way to be some-
> one else for a little while. It's really relaxing."
> — Anna, 16

What are your interests? Does your school offer something along those lines? If it doesn't, is there a community organization that does? Church? Something? School is about so much more than schoolwork. Get out there and learn about life.

I WANT TO GET A JOB. WHAT SHOULD I DO?

I got a job ten days after I turned sixteen, and I've been, for the most part, gainfully employed since then.

> "Working has helped my ability to talk with other
> people as I help customers and things. And I work
> at the mall, so that's fun, because I like being
> around a lot of people, and there are always people
> there." — Haden, 16

My first job was at a sub shop, where I was allowed to eat as many bags of chips and down as many soft drinks as I wanted — I had to pay only for sandwiches. I worked there a month and a half and got paid twice. Both times I had to ask for my check.

It was a weird sensation, working. I mean, I'd volunteered at church a million times, and this just felt like more of the same. I was pretty good at math and machines, so I was a natural at the cash register, and since I lived in a small town, I knew almost everyone who came in. It was nice. My parents actually had to remind me to ask for my checks — I forgot I was supposed to get paid.

To this day, I can't stand the smell of mozzarella cheese because of that job. One day, the owner backed into the front-most parking space and opened the trunk of his car. Inside? Two huge garbage bags (I'm sure they were clean) of shredded mozzarella. He directed me to remove the bags from the trunk, take them to the back, and transfer the contents into smaller bags that would then go into the freezer until they were needed.

I got to work, but hunkering over all that cheese, the sheer volume of it, made me gag. The smell was so strong, like the cheese had very long fingers that it was forcefully sticking into my nostrils, try as I might to prevent it.

These are the memories *you'll* be making soon!

A month and a half later, I became a "courtesy clerk" (read that as "sacker") for a grocery store. I liked it better, though I didn't care for the goofy dress shirt/black pants/apron combo I had to wear.

> "My job is something I love to do, but it definitely attacks my free time. I used to not be able to come to church or youth group, but I worked my schedule around that now. It's definitely a trade-off. The money helps, though." — Josh, 16

Anyway, there's a world of potential employment opportunities out there for a student like you — the question is whether you should take them.

I vote "yes."

First, as with all these things, check with your parents to make sure they're cool with it. If they are, I see nothing wrong—and everything right—with earning some extra cash in your spare time. This is what you're going to be doing your entire life; you might as well get a head start now.

Here are things you might learn while working:

- *That "taxes" are real*
- *How to be nice to customers*
- *How to be nice to your fellow employees*
- *How to be nice to your manager, especially if you want a raise in the near future*
- *That money is a tool and that just like it can be earned, it can also be blown*
- *Appreciation for what your parents do*

And that's just a small sample.

> "Having a job is a good and bad thing at the same time. Anytime anyone invites me to something, they don't give me enough advance notice. I gotta have eighteen days to get off from work, so you can't call me and say, 'Hey, you wanna go bowling or something?' Sure, I'd love to go bowling, but that's not the question. The question is 'Can I?' and the answer is 'No.'"—Grant, 17

You know what I did with my hard-earned cash? I bought CDs, fast food, and gas for my car so I could drive to work and make more hard-earned cash. It was kind of nice, and sort of a foreshadowing for my life now, though I've added a few things to the list of stuff I buy with my hard-earned cash.

Just be sure you're aware what you're getting into. A job at this time in your life should be more like a hobby—something you do every now and then. There's plenty of time for working full-time later. Take this time now to get your feet wet and learn how to enjoy the dollar or two you bring home.

And hope your parents don't start charging rent.

I LOVE COMPETITION, WHETHER IT'S IN SPORTS OR SOMETHING ELSE. IS THAT OKAY?

> "If you compete at doing something you love and you do well at it, it gives you a really good sense of self-worth." — Kaitlin, 17

I love competition too. In fact, I can be kind of a jerk about it. The other day we were playing a game as a family, and my team was me and two of my kids versus my wife and two of my other kids. My team had been in the lead the whole time when my wife's team got a question right and wound up moving ahead of us.

Overjoyed, my son, who is five, said, "Yeah, Dad! We're ahead of you now!"

You know what I said? "Enjoy it while it lasts, buddy!" I was good-natured about it, and I was half-kidding, but that means I was also half-serious—serious enough to trash-talk my five-year-old son (who took it all in stride, thankfully).

Also, we won the game.

Here's the thing: I don't think competition is a bad thing. I think quite the opposite—it's a great thing. Competition in sports leads not only to exciting games but also to the building of character traits in the players. Competition in the business world is what our entire economy is based on—businesses compete with each other to get your money.

> "I'm a really competitive person. I just like to beat people at things—I like to be number one. I don't know why. I just really like competition. It gets your adrenaline pumping a lot more than if you were just doing something to do it."—Anna, 16

Competition spurs on creativity, teaches the value of perseverance, and develops inner strength within us. It's a perfect way to practice getting through the hard times that life inevitably tosses our way.

But, with all that said, competition can go horribly wrong when we forget that it's just a game.

I coached my kids' soccer team one year, and that was a clinic in the proper usage of competition in life. The very first thing I taught the kids on the team (which was made up of five- and six-year-olds) was not the basics of soccer. I didn't go over dribbling or kicking or shin guards or any of that stuff. I let them know that the most important things on the field are all the other people.

So that's how we practiced. I taught them a few fundamentals, but I always made sure they understood that the people were more important than the ball. Especially since kids that age tend to bunch around the ball and, in a desperate attempt to get a foot on it, kick or push someone out of the way. Not so on *my* team, mister!

Anyway, at game time, I always gathered them around and reminded them that we were there to have fun with our friends and then kick the ball a little bit. I tried to work them all into the rotation so they all played the same amount of minutes, regardless of their skill level.

You can imagine how this killed me.

One week we played a team where the coach did not see it that way. His goal? To win. And not just to win—he wanted to clobber us. He instructed his kids to be extremely aggressive in the way they played. They didn't throw any elbows or anything, but they definitely took the ball to our side of the field quite a bit.

It was bad. I remember distinctly, we were losing 13-0 with about two minutes left to play (according to the rules, the ref should've called the game when we went down 11-0, I found out later), and we actually had the ball on their side of the field. One of my kids made a wild kick that sent the ball toward one of his kids, and the coach leapt up and down on the field screaming, "Go down! Go down!" and pointing toward our goal.

You would think that we were locked in some sort of epic battle that would be decided within the final seconds. This coach was treating it like a dramatic come-from-behind Super Bowl win instead of what it was: bad sportsmanship.

Winning got in the way.

And this happens all the time. Baseball player Barry Bonds owns a record for most career home runs, but instead of being celebrated for it, no one cares. Why? Because he's (allegedly) a cheater who scowled his way to the top. It was only once he got there that someone started to say it wasn't right.

But Bonds was always like that. Read up on his early career and you'll find that he had a bad attitude in high school. He had a bad attitude in college. He had a bad attitude in the minors, and in the majors. But he got away with it because he was too talented.

Winning got in the way.

We have a new scandal in the business world almost every

day because so many companies get focused on winning and on making money that they forget about trivial things like, I don't know, rules and laws.

It isn't wrong to try your best—not by any stretch of the imagination. The desire to do your best is a God-given one. But we must always, always remember that God's number-one mission for our lives is the other person. The other people.

People. That's where God's heart is, and it's where our hearts need to be as well.

WHAT CLASSES SHOULD I BE TAKING?

This is such a sticky question, because so much of it depends on what you want to do with the rest of your life. And *that* depends on whether you *know* what you want to do with the rest of your life. If you don't know, you're still in good shape.

There's a misconception that you *must* know the complete course of your entire life from the time you are, say, five years old. In the pressure of today's economy, with more people trying to get fewer jobs, there seems to be an attitude that says the more you think and plan ahead, the better off you'll be. So if you, by chance, or lack of foresight, haven't thought or planned ahead, some would tell you that you're behind the eight ball.

I think you're fine.

The Bible has a couple of mentions of this type of thinking, and if we read between the lines, we can figure out a good course of action for you. First, in Proverbs 21:5, the Bible says, "Careful planning puts you ahead in the long run; hurry and scurry puts you further behind."

So from that, it sounds like planning ahead is a great thing and that if you haven't done it, you're screwed.

Ah, but then we have James 4:13-15: "I have a word for you

who brashly announce, 'Today—at the latest, tomorrow—we're off to such and such a city for the year.
We're going to start a business and make a lot of money.'
You don't know the first thing about tomorrow. You're nothing but a wisp of fog, catching a brief bit of sun before disappearing. Instead, make it a habit to say, 'If the Master wills it and
we're still alive, we'll do this or that.'"

And from that, it sounds like planning ahead is . . . not so
smart.

So which to believe? How about both? Because the passage in
James lets us know that it isn't *wrong* to plan ahead—what's wrong
is assuming our plans are infallible and concrete. It's a good thing
to plan ahead; it's a bad thing to put our plans before God's.

With that in mind, what classes should you take? The best
way to determine that is to ask God what He would have you do
with your life, with your calling. Where do you feel God is sending you to work for His kingdom? Into the business world? The
creative world? The ever-expanding graphic design industry?
The mission field? The pastorate? Blue-collar ministry?

If you have an interest in acting, take theater classes. If you
have an interest in medicine, take biology. If you have an interest
in working with your hands, try out shop or, if your school has
it available, a vocational technology program. Look into other
activities that might pertain to something you want to do. Seek
assistance from your school's guidance counselors—that's why
they're there.

But in all of that, never forget that God's plans supersede
yours and that He may move you from one area of life to another,
unexpectedly and, sometimes, seemingly without reason. Just
never be afraid to go with Him—His will is always the smartest
way.

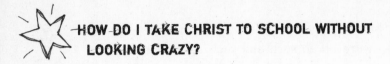

HOW DO I TAKE CHRIST TO SCHOOL WITHOUT LOOKING CRAZY?

Easy. You pack Him in your lunch box, right behind a thermos of tomato soup. That way, He's *your* little secret.

Wait. You probably don't use lunch boxes anymore, huh? Or thermoses? Those are *so* elementary school, and you aren't reading *The Elementary School Survival Guide: How to Avoid Getting Cooties and Eating Paste.*

Honestly, this is a question that plagues even us adults: How radical can we be before we blow our witness? For you, it's school. For us, it's work. It's a never-ending balance of living out your faith and living in the real world.

The question really boils down to authenticity. How authentic are you willing to let your life be? Do you want to pretend that since you're a Christian, everything is all roses and buttercups and lollipops and rainbows in your life? Or are you willing to let everyone else in and see that you have troubles just like they do?

Jesus made it plain that even if you are His disciple, you will have tough times. Jesus even said that very thing to His own disciples when He said, "In this godless world you will continue to experience difficulties" (John 16:33).

You're going to have problems. You're going to have difficulties, just like everyone at your school who *isn't* a Christian. But Jesus didn't leave it at that—He gave a solution to the problem of those difficulties we experience: "But take heart! I've conquered the world" (that's the rest of John 16:33).

Jesus has conquered the godless world that we walk in. That is what sets Christians apart from those who don't know Him—that the guy who conquered this world lives inside us and guides us and gives us strength to conquer it ourselves.

That is where we find our authenticity. And authenticity is

key to relating your faith to people without sounding weird. I always turn to a story in the book of John when I start to think about the idea of evangelizing without looking like a kook.

In the ninth chapter of John, Jesus heals a guy who was blind from birth, but He did it on the Sabbath day, so it caused a big stir among the Pharisees. They figured it wasn't right for Jesus to heal on the Sabbath, that He was breaking God's law and was therefore not of God.

So they truck this formerly blind dude into court and start to grill him about Jesus. "What is He? A prophet? An impostor? What?" And the guy, in verse 25, says something very disarming: "I know nothing about that one way or the other. But I know one thing for sure: I was blind . . . I now see."

That's all we need to do. We just need to tell people, "I was blind . . . I now see." Tell our story to others. Tell about Jesus—the way He changed our lives.

But we must relate it to the hearers. If we just broadcast Jesus all day long with no context, no way for them to see how He relates to them, then our broadcasting isn't going to have much impact. Our lives must connect the dots—sometimes *become* the connection—between Jesus and those around us who don't know Him.

Let's examine something in the life of Paul. In Acts 17:22-23, Paul is speaking to some people in Athens who are very dedicated to worship. They worship any and every god of their time, and then, just to make sure they have their bases covered, they have a shrine to an unknown god. Check out the way Paul breaks it down to them: "It is plain to see that you Athenians take your religion seriously. When I arrived here the other day, I was fascinated with all the shrines I came across. And then I found one inscribed, TO THE GOD NOBODY KNOWS. I'm here to introduce you to this God so you can worship intelligently, know who you're dealing with."

You see that? Paul didn't hop on a soapbox and start calling down the fire of God on them for worshipping false gods. Instead, he saw where they were, saw that their hearts were open to truth, and revealed that truth to them. He introduced them to God.

And surely, after Paul's authoritative speech, everyone listening rushed forward to accept Christ? Nope. He actually got a mixed reaction. We learn in verses 32-34 that "some laughed at him and walked off making jokes; others said, 'Let's do this again. We want to hear more.' But that was it for the day, and Paul left. There were still others, it turned out, who were convinced then and there, and stuck with Paul."

When you share your faith, you are not always guaranteed the type of reaction you want. No big deal. As long as you share it honestly, as an extension of the regular ol' life you're leading, you should be good. It's up to your listeners to decide what to do with the information you give them—it's only up to you to give it to them.

CHAPTER 5

YOU AND THE WORLD

My counsel for you is simple and straightforward: Just go ahead with what you've been given. You received Christ Jesus, the Master; now live him. You're deeply rooted in him. You're well constructed upon him. You know your way around the faith. Now do what you've been taught. School's out; quit studying the subject and start living it! And let your living spill over into thanksgiving. (Colossians 2:6-7)

If you decide for God, living a life of God-worship, it follows that you don't fuss about what's on the table at mealtimes or whether the clothes in your closet are in fashion. There is far more to your life than the food you put in your stomach, more to your outer appearance than the clothes you hang on your body. Look at the birds, free and unfettered, not tied down to a job description, careless in the care of God. And you count far more to him than birds. (Matthew 6:25-26)

Make the Master proud of you by being good citizens. Respect the authorities, whatever their level; they are God's emissaries for keeping order. It is God's will that by doing good, you might cure the ignorance of the fools who think you're a danger to society. Exercise your freedom by serving God, not by breaking the rules. Treat everyone you meet with dignity. Love your spiritual family. Revere God. Respect the government. (1 Peter 2:13-17)

I KNOW EVERYONE SAYS THEY'RE BAD, BUT WHAT'S UP WITH DRUGS AND ALCOHOL? CAN'T I HAVE A LITTLE FUN?

Since I was a kid, this world has been inundated with more antidrug and antialcohol (for the under-21 crowd, anyway) messages than I can count. For me, it started in the fifth grade, when a police officer came to my school and spoke about DARE and how it was the best and how drugs were the worst.

I remember in the sixth grade when my science teacher told us about the dangers of huffing from gas cans—I felt bad because I'd always liked the smell of gasoline when my dad would fill up the car, and I'd sometimes take a big whiff. I didn't know I'd been *doing drugs!* I repented and started holding my nose at the pump (which my mom later talked me out of).

I remember in the eighth grade when this ex–professional football player spoke to my school about the dangers of cocaine and how he'd done so much of it that the drug had eaten a hole in his septum (that wall between your nostrils) so he could pass a handkerchief from one nostril to the other. He didn't do it, but he said he could.

Point is, I've heard a bazillion stories about this stuff, and so have you. So, if that's the case, why are drugs still around? Why are students like you still dealing with the pressures of drinking or smoking or taking any other banned substance?

Why does it seem worse now than ever before?

I can't answer the why, but I can tell you that it's here. It exists. You know it, and I know it. You've probably dealt with this several times over already. Maybe you'd rather be drunk or high right now. Maybe you already are.

So why should you steer clear? Why should you swim against the current and say "no"?

Because I said so.

Also: God said so. Right there, in 1 Corinthians 6:19-20: "Didn't you realize that your body is a sacred place, the place of the Holy Spirit? Don't you see that you can't live however you please, squandering what God paid such a high price for? The physical part of you is not some piece of property belonging to the spiritual part of you. God owns the whole works. So let people see God in and through your body."

Throw aside the very compelling argument that drugs, alcohol, and smoking are all illegal (unless you're eighteen, in which case you can *legally* smoke) — their illegality is reason enough not to do it. No, we're tossing that aside for a higher purpose — the purpose that your body is not yours.

It's God's.

And He doesn't want you trashing it. Especially with stupid nonsense that's just going to trash your witness along with your body.

Look, there's an argument to be made here against trashing your body with crappy food, or with tattoos, or with crazy colors of hair dye, or with piercings, or anything else along those lines. But those things are all matters of lifestyle choice, and they aren't really associated with the party, I'm-trying-to-numb-the-pain-this-weekend mentality.

Drugs? Alcohol? Smoking?

All bearing connotations of relying on something other than God to make it through the day. People don't do drugs for the heck of it—they do them to forget their life, for a little while. The same goes (for most people) for drinking and smoking—these things take the edge off of life. They're used as coping mechanisms.

They're God replacements.

Which, as we know, doesn't work. God cannot be replaced. So anything you stick in there as an attempt is just going to fail. And fail big.

Don't turn to the boring ol' standards of everyone else. Stick with the real thing—stick with God. Honor Him, and He'll satisfy you in ways some chemical never will.

ISN'T THE INTERNET AWESOME?

Yes, it is. I love the internet. Too much, sometimes—it's such an easy distraction, what with MySpace and Facebook and YouTube and Homestar Runner cartoons and the zillion other wholesome destinations out there.

> "The internet is a massive time-waster. And now you can do it on mobile phones, too. It wastes so much time. And money." —Josh, 16

It's safe to say that the internet might be the greatest thing to happen to our culture in a long, long time. We've never been so connected to each other; we've never had these unprecedented opportunities to communicate with people so far away.

> "You can check your MySpace page three times in a row and expect to see something different. But I guess I'm not popular enough, because there's never a new comment. So I've had to stop wasting time with that. I'll check it once, and then, whatever, I'm good for another week." — Grant, 17

We've also never had the ability to sin, sin, sin like this. In private, on our own.

With no one watching.

Well, *almost* no one.

Pornography, raunchy message boards and chat rooms, profane blogs—you name it, it's out there. Page after page of material that would best remain unvisited. Chances are, if you've messed around on the internet for any amount of time, you've probably stumbled upon something, just through a typing error or a misplaced click.

So how do you guard against the potential evils of the internet? What if you've already been exposed to something sinful and are finding it hard to resist going back?

First things first: Tell someone. Tell your parents, tell your youth leader, tell a friend you can trust—just tell someone. This is huge. We're all in this together, and the Devil would love nothing more than to convince you otherwise—to tell you that you're the only one who struggles with this private sin.

You aren't.

Whatever it is, you aren't.

 So tell someone. Pick someone who will understand where you're coming from but will help you stay accountable as you move toward the future. If you're worried that your parents will freak out, tell a friend or youth worker first. Your folks need to know, but getting it off your chest to someone will help you as you talk to your parents about it.

Another major help in this area is to get your parents to invest in an internet filter. There are literally hundreds of programs out there, some free, some requiring a small monthly fee. Hopefully your parents have already activated some type of parental control on your home internet connection, but if they haven't, mention it to them. You can't be too careful, and the knowledge that someone else could retrace your steps will keep you out of trouble like nothing else will.

The internet is a marvelous invention, and one that will enrich our lives for years to come, but just like any other tool, we must use it for the proper purposes. Get others involved, and you'll go far toward staying clean.

AM I WHAT CULTURE SAYS I AM?

"Sometimes society just seems so overwhelming. I don't know what to do." — Jenava, 17

You may not realize this, but our culture is telling you things all the time. Mostly, it's telling you how to act, think, and feel. We live in a constant state of being advertised to, in magazines, signage at the mall, billboards, internet banner ads, television commercials, movie posters, those stupid preshow slides at the movies, those stupid commercials at the movies, within the movies themselves—it's everywhere.

And every single ad says one thing: "You are incomplete."

Think about it. They're all trying to convince you that you need whatever product or service they're offering. Sometimes they even exaggerate an affliction so they can then solve it (your acne is causing you to lose all your friends, your jeans are so yesterday, your hair color really should change to explain your mood, if you don't have an iPhone no one will talk to you).

The message is everywhere. Feel incomplete? It's because you need our soda / makeup / tanning cream / coffee / landscaping / computer program / ab workout system / charcoal / groceries / overpriced sport utility vehicle / underpriced frozen pizzas. You get the idea.

I used to work in the advertising world—I know exactly how it goes. The key word there is "FAB." That's an acronym standing for "Features And Benefits." The idea is this: In your advertising, you talk about a particular feature of this particular underpriced frozen pizza (sauce in the crust!) and then you make the connection for the audience as to *how* that feature will benefit them directly (it's a taste explosion!) and therefore why they need to buy *your* underpriced frozen pizza instead of all the other underpriced frozen pizzas in their grocer's freezer (the only one with sauce in the crust!).

> "It's **impossible** not to **feel pressure from the culture** to look a certain way, act a certain way. Everything is 'more,' and it's presented as something you want. You go to a store and there are signs saying, 'Just what you want, we're having a sale, 50% off so you can get one more!' Let's make this iPod, and then we'll make a bigger iPod, and then we'll make a video iPod, and then we'll make an iPod phone. It just keeps growing. Our society is based on having more."
> —Jenava, 17

Every ad is like this. Every single one. Oftentimes they end with what is known as a "call to action" in order to get you to do something tangible (visit underpricedfrozenpizza.com to taste our sauce for yourself!) so they can then sell you on more stuff.

Even this book was advertised in the same way. There's a hip cover that maybe caught your eye, and a clever synopsis on the back written by someone in the marketing department at TH1NK to show you the features and benefits of the book and, maybe not overtly, the reason you need to read it. Don't believe me? Flip it over and check it out for yourself.

See what I mean? I don't know that because I read the back cover—that copy was written well after I typed this sentence. It's just the way it works.

There is one type of advertisement that isn't as bad as the rest, and this is called the "image ad." This is one of those ads, usually related to a cause or movement, that doesn't promote a particular product but instead talks about the cause or movement and then ends with maybe a logo or innocuous phrase to let you know who paid for the ad (Stamp out illiteracy—brought to you by your local library . . . and Underpriced Frozen Pizza. Dot com.).

There's a reason I'm going on and on about our current system of advertising and marketing, and it really does have to do with you. I want you to see that our culture is purposely sending you a very true message, but with the wrong solution: You need help, and you need it from *us*.

Now, I don't see anything wrong with advertising in and of itself. After all, there's no other way, really, to get your message out there about your product, and the buying and selling of products and services is what makes our world go 'round. There are many commercials and other ads I actively enjoy, if they're creative and well thought-out.

"I'm not a big fan of culture, honestly. Just being in our culture — I despise it. I hate what we spend our time on. I don't like that I can't go a day without being tempted by some billboard with a half-naked woman on it. It's just so prevalent. I can't go a day without seeing something halfway repulsive." — Grant, 17

But we must realize the underlying message of most advertising and counter it with the truth of God's Word. And God's Word says this: You need help, and you need it from God.

See the difference?

You are not what our culture says you are. Our culture says you're broken and you need a cultural fix. You are broken, for sure, but you need a spiritual fix.

And this fix gives back so much more than it costs.

WHAT ABOUT MY CLOTHES? THE MUSIC I LISTEN TO? THE MOVIES OR TV SHOWS I WATCH? HOW MUCH OF THAT STUFF STICKS WITH ME?

Welcome to yet another thorny topic, especially the movies/music question. Different parents have different rules for this stuff. When I was growing up, I pretty much didn't watch any movie that wasn't on broadcast television, and the most "out there" music I was allowed to have was anything by Carman.

My wife, on the other hand, listened to anything and everything and could watch just about any movie she wanted to. Fortunately for her, she never wanted to watch anything, since she doesn't care much about movies, so she was pretty good there.

So, first and foremost, you need to honor your parents' rules about this stuff. If, for example, they've laid down the law about what you can and cannot wear, listen to them. Respect them. Whether you agree with them or not, you need to follow through on their requests, simply because they're your parents.

But what if your folks are more lax in what they allow you to wear and see? You'll probably want to take a tour of the Bible and find a Scripture to figure out where you need to draw the line.

Why, turns out I have one right here! "Summing it all up, friends, I'd say you'll do best by filling your minds and meditating on things true, noble, reputable, authentic, compelling, gracious — the best, not the worst; the beautiful, not the ugly; things to praise, not things to curse" (Philippians 4:8).

I don't want to get into a big list of dos and don'ts — I think you're smart enough to judge these things for yourself — but this passage does give you some nice criteria for comparison. Wondering if that one song from that artist you like is something you should listen to? Hold it up to this passage and see how it fits.

Curious about the next big blockbuster movie that's going to open this weekend? Check the passage.

What about that one website everyone seems to visit? You got it: the passage.

And that outfit? The passage.

It's a good rule of thumb for your entire media intake: If it fits Philippians 4:8, it should be fine. If it doesn't, maybe you'll help yourself by chucking it aside. Sure, that one movie may not send you sliding into sin, but we're not talking about how you'll do *worst* — these suggestions are simply the way you'll do *best*.

Because the bad stuff? The stuff mentioned here? It

does stick with you. Before I regulated my movie watching (can you tell I like movies? Sorry I keep talking about them), I would watch pretty much anything that hit the theaters, especially if it had any sort of critical buzz around it. And in that time, I saw some crazy stuff on the screen.

And I still have those images with me. They don't invade my daily thoughts; I don't have to deal with them all the time. But sitting here, right now, telling you this, I can see about three, four, five scenes from different movies that I wish I'd never seen. Things that *definitely* don't fit the criteria of being true, noble, reputable, authentic, compelling, or gracious.

> "One thing I hate about our culture is that we say we want everything to be of higher quality, but so many things that become popular are so mediocre. Especially books and music. There are things that everybody likes for no reason other than they're told to like it." — Phil, 14

Same thing goes for music. There have been entire books written about the evils of any music that isn't a southern gospel quartet, and I certainly don't want to go down *that* road, but I will say that music sticks with you in ways other things can't. It does speak directly to your soul, often bypassing your brain in the process, so you should be careful about what you put in there.

You know that song "I Will Always Love You" by Whitney Houston? I will forever associate that song with a teenage crush I had. Why? Because I was at a high school dance, and there was a girl I'd liked for a long time, and I was finally going to get up the nerve to ask her to dance with me — until that song came on and I saw her dancing and making out with another guy.

I still can't listen to that song without feeling that emotional hurt. I mean, I'm completely over it at this point (and, truth be told, now that I'm older and wiser, thankful that I hadn't pursued anything with that girl—she was definitely *not* God's best for me), but I still feel that twinge of betrayal anytime Whitney starts belting the heck out of the letter "I."

Music is powerful. That's why God invented it. Visual images are powerful. That's why God invented them. Keep these things in mind as you make your way through our cultural landscape and you'll be just fine.

HEY, I'M JUST A TEENAGER—CAN I MAKE A DIFFERENCE IN THE WORLD?

Many, many people would love to tell you that because you're young, you can't make a difference in the world. This is not new. The apostle Paul said something about it to young Timothy when he wrote, "Don't let anyone put you down because you're young" (1 Timothy 4:12). Obviously, the world has always been prejudiced against its own youth.

> "If you have the drive, if you have the passion for what you're standing up for, then it can be done." — Kat, 17

But the youth of history have always risen to the challenge. We see this in the Bible most obviously with the story of David, who, as a youth, took out the giant Goliath, and we also see it in 2 Kings 22, when the eighteen-year-old king of Judah, Josiah, changed his nation.

Judah, which was an offshoot of the nation of Israel between the time of David and Jesus, had really gotten bad. All kinds of idol worship had sprung up, even to the point of taking over God's temple. Yep, people were worshipping idols—in a temple that had been built specifically for God.

How had this happened? They'd lost the written Word of God. Misplaced it. It was there, in the temple, but it had been lost. One day, Josiah decided the temple needed to be renovated, so he sent some folks down there to get started. And they found the Book of the Law, the part of the Bible that had been written up to that point. They scuttled that sucker over to Josiah pronto, and after he read it, he knew the whole nation had messed up severely.

So he turned the nation around, back to God. He tore down every single idol, every single shrine—everything that had been erected to worship a god that wasn't Jehovah, the God of the Israelites. He removed all of it and renewed Judah's covenant with God.

And he was a teenager.

Want some more examples? You know the Braille system of raised bumps that allows blind people to read? That was invented by a fifteen-year-old kid named Louis Braille. C. S. Lewis, perhaps the most influential Christian writer of the twentieth century, began forming his ideas for the land of Narnia in his teens, writing and learning various forms of mythology that would inform his later creation.

Can you make a difference? You bet.

We all affect the world around us. There's no telling what sort of impact you will have on someone. I pursued the guitar because a classmate of mine knew how to play this really cool song that I wanted to learn (mainly because I thought it would make girls like me). I'd tried to learn guitar a few times before that, but it never stuck until this kid played that song for me when I was a junior in high school.

Turns out guitar playing changed my life. In college, I got in a band, we found this cute girl singer, and I wound up marrying her.

That kid? He changed the course of my life without even knowing it.

So what are you doing? How are you having a positive impact on the world? On your world? On the people around you?

> "Making a **difference in the world is easier if** you do it in a group setting. Only a **few select people will believe** an individual, but if you have a group of people all saying the same thing, you're more likely to get **people to listen to you.**" — Tyler, 17

Listen, no single person is going to change the world in a single day. There are a lot of hurting people out there, and you aren't going to be able to reach them all. But you can reach the ones right next to you. You can change *their* world, and in the process, you can start to change *this* world.

DO I HAVE TO GO TO CHURCH TO BE A CHRISTIAN?

In order to fully answer this question, we first have to set some ground rules as to what, exactly, do we mean by the word *church*?

The Bible speaks of "the church" not as a building but as an organism, a living thing. When you become a Christian, you don't have to *go* to church — you *are* the church. You become part of the body of Christ. You become the church, or at least a part of the larger group of people who've also become Christians.

However, that doesn't mean you suddenly have all you need to live a godly life. Look through the Bible, especially the New Testament, and you'll see that the early Christians—and Jesus Himself—were organized into an association. No one did their own thing. No one went solo.

Paul went on many missionary journeys to preach the gospel, yes, but also to establish groups of believers in one city. His letters, which make up some two-thirds of the New Testament, were letters written to churches about certain topics they were dealing with. These early churches were vital to the growth of Christianity.

Even Jesus had a church gathering, of sorts, if you look at the disciples. He had a group of guys who helped Him out, learned at His feet, ran errands for Him (they fetched the colt He rode into Jerusalem in Matthew 21:6), handed out food (during the feeding of the five thousand in Luke 9:14), and practiced their own faith (Peter walking on water in Matthew 14:24-31).

And after Jesus died, these disciples—Peter especially—formed the backbone of the early church.

Paul, when he went on his missionary journeys, never went alone. He went out with Barnabas (Acts 11:30), then was joined by John, who also went by the name of Mark (Acts 12:25). Paul and Barnabas were then joined by Silas and a dude named Judas (Acts 15:22), who was a different Judas from the one who betrayed Jesus. Shortly afterward, Paul and Barnabas got into a heated discussion about the work ethic of John/Mark, and they split up. Paul chose to carry on with Silas (Acts 15:40) and then a young guy named Timothy (Acts 16:1-3).

Sorry for all the references, but I just wanted you to see that in the early church, it was important for even the biggest of leaders to have someone in his corner.

I have a friend who is fond of saying that "faith was never meant to be done alone," and I can't think of a better way of expressing it. We're all in this together, this life. We need each other.

HOW IMPORTANT IS MY YOUTH GROUP?

I like to think of life as a walk. We are all, if we are living, walking along the path of our life, and every choice we make changes the direction of our path, our walk, our "journey," as so many reality-show contestants like to put it. And sometimes our paths cross with other people's paths, and sometimes our paths run parallel to other people's, like they do with our parents or siblings or, later in life, our spouses.

So imagine with me, if you will, this path. Imagine that you're walking along this path in a quiet meadow, perhaps surrounded by a field of wildflowers or something else tranquil—whatever makes you feel calm.

Now imagine that your path suddenly comes up to a steep mountain—a big rocky mass jutting right into your path, with all sorts of sharp prominences and outcroppings and jagged pieces of stone stuck in your way. But your path leads straight up that stupid mountain, so if you're going to go on with life, you have to get over the mountain.

Are you still tracking with me? Okay, good. Now, let me ask you this question: Would you rather tackle that mountain on your own, or would you rather tackle it with someone else, someone who can lend a hand to help you over it, someone who maybe has been rock climbing before, or even just someone who gives you another set of eyes on those danger-ous slopes?

> "My youth group has been my counterweight. I get really spiritually depressed at my school, and then I go to youth group and I feel like it's okay to be doubting, it's okay to be questioning and honest, and it's okay to not be perfect." — Hanna, 16

What if you could go over it with a whole *group* of people? Ten, fifteen, twenty people who all are helping you to get over that mountain? Wouldn't that be better than trying to do it on your own?

This is life with your youth group. It's always good to have a group of friends to surround you when you hit life's mountains — and for you to surround when *they* hit one. But there's something special about a group that is on the same spiritual journey as you. It's one thing to have friends whose paths line up with yours; it's something entirely different when those friends have a spiritual element that mirrors yours.

When you go to youth group, you aren't just hanging out — you're lining up your path with the paths of other people and sharing the same spiritual instruction, the same teaching, and the same worship experiences. And because you're sharing so much with this group of people, you can help each other out when the mountains of life inevitably rear their ugly heads.

Do you mind if I switch metaphors really quickly? Thanks. In the Bible, in Proverbs 27:17, the writer put it this way: "You use steel to sharpen steel, and one friend sharpens another." Without any way to sharpen, a steel tool will quickly get dull as it's used; but when it interacts with other steel, it becomes sharper so it can be used longer and more effectively.

Don't minimize the importance of sharpening, of inviting other people to walk along the same path as you. It is the way we get through this life: together.

CHAPTER 6

YOU AND HAPPILY EVER AFTER

Skilled living gets its start in the Fear-of-God, insight into life from knowing a Holy God. It's through me, Lady Wisdom, that your life deepens, and the years of your life ripen. Live wisely and wisdom will permeate your life; mock life and life will mock you. (Proverbs 9:10-12)

Mortals make elaborate plans, but God has the last word. (Proverbs 16:1)

Don't for a minute envy careless rebels; soak yourself in the Fear-of-God —That's where your future lies. Then you won't be left with an armload of nothing. (Proverbs 23:17-18)

WHAT ARE COLLEGES LOOKING FOR, ANYWAY?

> "I don't think about college. I'm still a kid. I want to have fun. I have an idea what I want to do, but I haven't planned it out." — Kat, 17

This question is more loaded than Elmer Fudd's shotgun. There's no solid answer, as far as directing you to take this subject over that subject. That's why you (hopefully) have a guidance counselor on staff at your school — that person can definitely help you fulfill any credit requirements you might need.

It helps to know what college you're hoping to attend. If you want to head to a state school, you probably need only the standard requirements; if you're thinking of a private university or specialty school (like film school or Bible college), you might want to slant your schedule in favor of those pursuits.

What if you don't know what school you want to attend? What if (gasp!) you have no idea what to do with your life? Are you sunk? Hardly. You're actually in pretty good company — many, many people don't really know what they're "going to do" while in high school. I certainly hadn't planned on being a writer (truth be told, I was going to be a meteorologist until my senior year, at which time I switched to doing something in film or TV).

You also have the distinct benefit of living in a culture that values individuality like never before. Most of my friends are self-employed, freelance workers (mostly in writing, producing, and graphic design) who earn their living one job at a time. It used to be that if you wanted to achieve white-collar success (meaning not do manual labor for a living but rather work in the business world), you worked for a company behemoth.

> "I want to go to college, but I kind of don't want to go. You have to go to get a good education to get good money, but then I don't want to go to college and have to do all that work and have to go to more school, and then it's like school never ends. But then I want to get a good job and have good money. But then money isn't everything. It's hard to know what I want."
> — Marley, 15

But not these days. In fact, more people work for (or own) small businesses than work for the big dogs. The small business and the independent contractor are more accepted than ever before—you don't have to have a huge name to back you up anymore; you just have to do good work.

Just for fun, though, let's assume you want to work for a regular ol' company—one of those big suckers that gets traded on the New York Stock Exchange. Fortunately, it's extremely achievable, especially if you know what you want to do for them. You can pursue that avenue as far as you can in high school. Find out what college their CEO attended. Their CFO. Their COO. Their VPs. Is that school a possibility for you? Pursue it.

Now that you know what school you want to attend, you have a much better shot at focusing your remaining high school career on getting into that school. Contact the university; find out what requirements they look for in a student. Does their admissions office give any extra weight to extracurricular activities? Do they look for certain subjects? Are you on the right track to getting there?

Another thing to consider is whether the school of your choice gives any merit to AP classes. Most colleges do, but some of them treat AP testing differently from other schools, offering three hours of college credit where others may offer only one (or none at all). These are things you definitely want to check out before you bank your college career on acing that AP exam.

But what if you have no clue what you're going to do with your life? What if the only thing you're sure of is that you intend to spend it breathing? Not a problem.

> "I don't want to **decide** my **college** major yet. I want to go **my freshman year** and try out **all these different** things. I've always been interested in medicine, and I've liked theater and archaeology. I want to take **different** classes and see what I really want to do **with my life.**"
> — Jennifer, 17

Like I said earlier, you're not the only person in that boat. And it's actually a pretty decent boat to be in, especially if you have a community or junior college nearby. Community college is perfect for those who don't know exactly what they want to do. It's even good for those who *do* know, if only because that tends to change once you're actually in school.

Why's it so good? Well, it isn't as prestigious as heading off to Harvard like your school's valedictorian, but it's a much less expensive way to get all your standard subjects out of the way. In the college experience, you're always going to have certain subjects that have nothing to do with your major: English, humanities, basic math, probably one of the sciences. Community college is a great opportunity for taking those classes at a reduced price so that, should you go on to a regular university, you can focus your time and money on the classes that pertain to your major.

No, it isn't cool, but it makes sense, as uncool stuff often does. When I was in high school, there was no way I would've gone to junior college, but now that I've lived some life after the fact (and *finally* paid off my college loans), I can see that a couple of years at junior college would've done me very, very well.

HOW SHOULD I STUDY FOR THOSE BIG COLLEGE ENTRANCE TESTS LIKE THE SAT OR THE ACT?

Okay, first things first. These tests, while important, are not the be-all/end-all of your life. As with most stuff in high school, you have to have a healthy perspective on their importance. It's very easy to distort their overall meaning until they become these huge *things* that lurk in every corner of your brain, never allowing you a moment's rest.

"I already know where I want to go. I want to go to a university that is two hours away so I can still come home on the weekends. But my mom already has everything planned out for me. I'm doing ACT prep this summer." — Gabrielle, 16

The SAT and the ACT *are* indeed important, but they aren't necessary for life. Again, a less-than-perfect score isn't going to draw an alien meteor into your living room. You will go on breathing. You will be able to digest your food, just like normal.

Your growth will not be stunted.

Not to minimize any anxiety you might be feeling. That anxiety is real, but there's a way to get through it without letting it paralyze you. And that way is through practice.

Yes, it pays to practice taking a test. I know, it seems strange, but think about it: This is important to your academic career, so it makes sense to give it a few dry runs instead of going in cold. At the risk of stating the obvious, look at it this way: If you were going to compete in some sort of an athletic competition, you wouldn't just show up one day with zero preparation. You'd practice, and you'd practice hard.

Same goes for the SAT and ACT. There are tons of practice tests available out there; pick some up and try them out. Just be sure to budget ample time to practice *before* your scheduled exam. You don't want to burn out your brain taking a practice exam the day before the real thing.

A lot of students get anxious about the timed part of the SAT and ACT. That always gave me a stomachache. But your life in the adult world is a series of deadlines and due dates, and the SAT and ACT are just hyped-up versions of that. Might as well learn to tackle it now.

When you take those practice exams, take them on the clock. Set a timer (preferably not one that ticks right next to your ear—that will only heighten the tension and provide a *constant* reminder of the passing time). The big thing to remember is not to let yourself get stuck on a particular question. This is really difficult for me, because if I can't figure something out, it stays with me, almost obsessively. It becomes this big obstacle that I *must* overcome in order to move on with my life.

But skipping the hard questions will almost always pay off in the long run, especially on the SAT, where a wrong answer actually affects your score. The SAT scoring system awards you a full point for every correct answer but deducts a fraction of a point for every incorrect answer. If you leave something blank, you get zero. So, to break it down:

right = positive points
wrong = negative points
blank = no points

This is why it's handy to learn how to skip the tough questions. You may spend a lot of time on one question only to get it wrong and lose points when you could've skipped it, using that time to answer more easy questions that you know you'll get right.

As for the ACT, there's no scoring system like that in place. If you get a question right, you get points. If you get it wrong or leave it blank, you get nothing. Still, it's good to answer the easy questions first, the ones you know, and come back to the hard ones later.

"So many people freak out about college. Some people say you have to plan out your entire high school career in, like, seventh grade. That's absolutely ridiculous. I'm an indecisive person, and my idea of what I want to do changes 24-7 almost. I have friends who've taken the SAT and the ACT ten times each, and they keep saying, 'We gotta get better,' even though they've gotten a great score. And they only study. To me, high school is supposed to be a fun experience, where you learn about life. You are supposed to be preparing for college, but to try to plan out your life is ridiculous. It doesn't work out like that." — Jenava, 17

So when you're practicing for
the tests, set your timer and do your
best to finish your practice tests in the
appropriate amount of time. If you suc-
ceed, give yourself a fun reward like a snack
or time off to watch *American Idol*.

Let's talk about the individual sections of the tests.
Both the SAT and the ACT have English and math sections,
but the ACT is completely multiple-choice; the SAT features a
written essay and math problems you must solve on your own.
(By the way, that wacky SAT scoring system doesn't come into
play on those non-multiple-choice math problems. You won't be
penalized with a wrong answer there, so do your best to answer
all of 'em.)

On the SAT, you'll find sections for sentence completion,
reading comprehension, that blasted written essay, the multiple-
choice math problems, and the other math problems. Just pace
yourself and you'll do fine — no need to worry about rushing
through and missing stuff you might otherwise get right.

Some tips: When you get to the sentence-completion section,
try to complete each sentence in your mind *before* looking at the
answers — believe it or not, it'll help you find the correct answer
as opposed to trying out the different multiple-choice options. Be
on the lookout for qualifying words that change the meanings of
sentences (the most obvious one is "not"), and pay attention to the
words on either side of the blank. Those will be your main clues
as to what answer you should choose.

On to reading comprehension: Read the whole passage
before you head over to the questions. I know it *feels* like you're
wasting time that way, but you aren't. It's really the smartest way
to proceed. While you're reading, just take in the information
without trying to memorize anything in particular — you'll tackle

the questions better that way.

Your written essay needs to be the standard academic essay: intro, three-paragraph body, and conclusion. Be sure to include your three main points in your introduction and sum up those points in your conclusion. Don't get too academic or too casual—just stick to simple language (and vary your sentence structure to look extra-smart—throw in a few complex sentences and you'll seem like a genius!) and you'll be fine.

The temptation on the multiple-choice math section is to work the problem halfway in an effort to make one of the selected answers fit. Even worse, there's a temptation to pick an answer and backtrack to see if it's the correct one. Avoid these temptations—they're time-wasters. Just work the problem to come up with the best response. And remember to do the easy ones first.

Okay, so those are the bones of the SAT. What about the ACT? This is a slightly different animal, but the essence remains the same: Answer the easy ones first, then the hard ones. If you're running low on time, just guess—you have a one-in-four chance of getting the correct answer, and you won't get penalized if you get one wrong.

On the ACT, you'll find sections on English, math, reading, and science. Be sure to read the directions for each section because the math section is the only one where you have to give the "correct" answer. The other sections try to trip you up by telling you to provide the "best" answer, meaning you have to read all the answers before giving yours. Oh, those sneaky ACT exam writers.

So you have the English section, which is basically just a lot of reading and trying stuff out to see what sounds best. Remember, you're not going for the "correct" answer—you're going for the "best" one, determined, of course, by what the ACT people think is "best." Just use the one that fits the writing style surrounding the blank.

You get to use a calculator on the math section, but don't use it as a crutch on the easy questions—you'll just be burning time unwisely. Break out the calculator when the going gets tough, and rely on your brain (and your fingers—I do it) for the rest of it. Again, as with the SAT, don't try to backtrack from the chosen answers. Just work the problem and pick the right one.

As evidenced by the book in your hand, you know how to read already, so the reading section should be a breeze. Just read the passage, then answer the questions. You can even go back to the passage and use it to verify the "best" answers. Not a problem.

The science portion can get a bit tricky because sometimes you have to consider two different scientific points of view. Again, you just have to be sure to read the material carefully and take notes if you have to. Remember: You're picking that arbitrary "best" answer.

So those are the basics of the two tests. The last thing to remember is to get plenty of rest the night before you take the test and to eat a hearty, healthy breakfast before you go. Don't eat anything too greasy or heavy—just some eggs and plain oatmeal or fresh fruit on some non-sugar cereal (i.e., *not* powdered donuts on your Lucky Charms). You want to give your body and brain fuel for the challenge ahead, and rest and healthy eating will do just that.

Once you've completed your test, blow off some steam in whatever way suits you best. For me, I'd pick up the guitar or go to a movie or call up some friends for a pickup basketball game. You know best how you like to relax, and you've just accomplished a major milestone in your life, so don't be afraid to kick back and celebrate. You've earned it.

OKAY, SMART GUY, HOW DO I PAY FOR ALL THIS "COLLEGE" STUFF?

Well, the simple answer: Have rich parents. Rich grandparents will also suffice.

So, that takes care of, like, 1 percent of the readers of this book. The rest of us have to come up with more creative solutions, many of which are out there — you just have to find them.

I'm going to level with you here (well, I'll level with you everywhere, so I guess that shouldn't be much of a surprise that I'm doing it here): The main way people pay for college is through student loans, and, if I may be frank, they suck.

Student loans could possibly be from the Devil.

Student loans are evil.

Student loans should be your last resort.

"But Adam, I'll have to get a loan because I don't have the grades to get a scholarship." Is that what you're thinking? Don't be fooled.

There are literally *thousands* of scholarships out there that apply to you. I'm not exaggerating, either. The number is in the thousands. Most of them offer only two or three thousand dollars, give or take a few hundred bucks, which certainly isn't going to set you up at Yale. But there is no law that says you can use only one scholarship in your pursuit of a higher education. You don't have to pick a single scholarship and ride that all the way to your diploma. You can use two, three, ten, twenty scholarships — as many as you receive, you can use. (I'm speaking generally, of course. If a particular university gives you a scholarship, you have to use it for that university, obviously. But I think you're catching my overall point, which is that you can add up several small scholarships to make one big one.)

What if you did this: Spend the summer before your senior year applying for as *many* scholarships as you can find. Anything that you remotely qualify for, apply for it. Even if you don't meet all the criteria for it, apply for it. You'd be surprised at which ones you'll get.

Apply for any and every scholarship, except any that require an up-front "processing fee" or anything like that. Those are scams; steer clear. (This also applies to anyone who approaches you on the street and tells you that you should be a model, gives you a card, and then tries to sell you 8x10 portraits — they just want your picture money. That's a free tip from me to you.)

If you already have a university in mind, be sure to apply for any scholarships that apply to that university. If you've already been accepted to a particular school, *definitely* inquire about any and all scholarships they might have.

Another avenue that isn't for everyone: paying through a work-study program, usually offered by the university you attend. This is an arrangement where you work for the university in some capacity (like in the library, or the campus store, or the campus post office or telecommunications office), but instead of getting paid actual money, you get a certain amount of scholarship money.

One of the benefits of using a work-study program is that you generally don't have to maintain a certain GPA in order to keep your scholarship. Most school-sponsored scholarships, at least those offered for academic merits, carry strict requirements with them. If you're GPA drops below a certain level, your scholarship can be reduced or even withdrawn entirely. Be sure to check with your school so you know the requirements ahead of time.

You can also pay for school the old-fashioned way: with actual money that you actually earn at an actual job. That's how I paid for the majority of my college learning. Well, it was a combination of that, along with a savings account my parents started for me when I was but a young tyke filled with enough promise to produce a writer but not enough to produce a full ride anywhere.

My first year in school, I'd combined my savings account money with my scholarship money to pay for that year, in cash, up front. I avoided extra cost by living off-campus in my house with my parents and by packing my lunch with groceries my mom bought instead of paying five bucks for mass-produced food that reminded me heavily of every summer camp mess hall I'd ever eaten in.

But in year two, my scholarship was no longer good and my savings account was depleted. All I had was my regular job money, and that wasn't enough to pay for the whole school year. So I did the unthinkable.

I got a loan.

It was a last resort, like I said.

Perhaps I'm being a little hard on the student loan, since those loans did help me complete my school on time. And, truth be told, student loans are offered at a very inexpensive interest rate that, unlike your standard credit card, doesn't shoot up twenty percentage points if you miss a payment. Most financial guru-type people agree that, as an adult, if you're carrying a lot of debt, pay off your student loans last—they're doing the least amount of damage.

I guess this is where I land on student loans: They are often a necessary evil, because while they allow you to go to school, they also stay with you for a long, long time. I have good friends who graduated from college more than ten years ago and are still paying off student loans. And that was just with a standard four-year bachelor's degree.

I did school the wrong way, personally. That second year, "The Year of the Loan," was for a four-year school where I was majoring in film. I was going to make movies, and I was going to have the film degree to prove it. Midway through that year, however, God tapped me on the shoulder and said, "What are you doing here?" I plugged my ears. Then the university dropped their film program after meeting with the alumni and realizing that none of their film graduates was working in film.

Suddenly I was a TV major at an expensive private four-year university. Then that tap came again: "What are you doing here?" I decided to give Him a listen.

God directed me to a small, cheap state school that, at the time, wasn't even a full-blown university. The best degree I could get was a two-year degree, what's called an associate's degree. I pulled up my stakes from the private university and headed to the small school to get, essentially, a two-year degree in three years.

Very smart.

However, since that school was so inexpensive, I was able to pay cash for my final year, which meant I'd taken out loans for only one of my three years of schooling. Not bad, right? Guess how long it took me to pay off that year.

Come on, guess.

Five years.

Now, that five years does include the initial six-month deferment (a "deferment" just means that you don't have to pay the loan for a while—but usually the interest keeps accumulating, so you wind up paying more in the long run anyway). It also includes another six-month deferment from a time when my wife and I were lucky to have two quarters to scrape together in order to generate a little heat.

Still, five years. For one year of schooling.

Sorry to give you the story of my life here, but I do think it's important that you understand what you're in for when you sign up for that student loan. You are signing your name to a debt you will be toting around for a long, long time. If you can avoid the student loan, please do.

HOW CLOSELY WILL MY COLLEGE EXPERIENCE MIRROR MY HIGH SCHOOL EXPERIENCE?

"I'm really excited about college. It's more of a hands-on type of learning, where you get the actual experience of performing in the field you want. Plus, you live there." — Anna, 16

Boy, this is a tough question, because so much depends on what you put into your college experience. There's just a lot going on when you hit college. Most students are away from home for the first time; your professors won't hold your hand nearly as much as your high school teachers do (it may not *seem* like it, but your high school teachers are holding your hand, compared to the treatment you'll get from most college professors); classes are harder; grades are determined by far less busywork; you have all kinds of interpersonal challenges, what with roommates and tons of fellow students from different parts of the country; and all the freedom can go to your head if you aren't remotely self-disciplined.

Whew. That was a mouthful.

College is, for the most part, not at all like thirteenth grade in high school—which is why you need to make the most of your high school experience while you can. It's really the last time in your life you'll have that particular type of experience. And not to scare you off of college, because it's great unto itself, but it is really like nothing you've done before.

Let's take 'em one at a time, starting with the home life. Now, I realize not everyone's home life is the same, by any stretch of the imagination, but there are a few things that I think remain constant, no matter how crazy or normal your life is at home. For starters, in high school, whether you like them or not, your fellow students share a lot of the same experiences as you. Some of you have grown up together, in the same city/town. You share a lot of the same memories. You probably know a lot of people from church and have known them for a while. You eat at the same restaurants; you hit up the same arcades. You're familiar with their parents and siblings. You're all coming at life from approximately the same direction, geographically.

> **"The college experience gives you a feeling of independence, a taste of what it's going to be like as an adult." — Jaime, 15**

In college, you're mainly surrounded by strangers who come from all different walks of life. It's intriguing, yet when you run into someone who speaks your same geographic language, you hold on to them for dear life. There's just something about having a friend or acquaintance who understands the regional differences — and those differences, whether you notice them or not, are there.

I'm sure you have tons of tough teachers in high school. There's no doubt they exist — teachers who are demanding, strict, unfair, and even (possibly) downright rude. But no matter how bad the teacher (and anytime you get in trouble, it's *always* the unfairness of the teacher and *never* anything you did, right?), there is a distinct difference between the high school instructor and his/her collegiate counterpart.

For starters, your high school teacher most likely gives you buckets of homework. Depending on the subject, you might even get homework every night, and all that homework goes toward determining your final grade once you've completed the class.

Not so in college, where your grade is generally determined by two to three exams throughout the semester and then a big final exam at the end of the semester. And . . . that's about it. All that busywork that contributes to your grade now? Forget it. It is a thing of the past when you hit higher education. Whether you think this is good or not is up to you.

In general, college professors treat you as an adult—they assume you are intelligent and disciplined enough to take proper notes on their (often long-winded) lectures and to actually read your textbooks.

I was not aware of this. I got through high school with copious note taking, and that's about it. I never read the books unless it was required for some sort of quiz (or, for the math stuff, to find whatever problems I had to solve). When I got to college, I figured note taking would be enough—until I took my first humanities (a highfalutin' name for "history") exam and realized that half the questions on the exam had come from a textbook I had never opened.

This is how I lost my scholarship.

"But I'm not in college, Adam," you might say. "I'm in high school. Duh. Why are you telling me all this stuff about college?" Oh, there's a reason.

If you know what you're going to get into, if you know that life as you know it (or are about to know it, depending on where you are in your high school career) will change, then you can better appreciate where you currently are. One of the worst feelings in life is regret—that feeling where you look back and think, *If only I'd known how little time I had in this situation, I would've done things differently.*

It's important that we take advantage of the time we have, and the only time we have is *now* (see James 4:13-15).

Jesus encountered a would-be disciple who wanted to get some stuff straightened out at home before following the Lord. Here's what Jesus said to him, found in Luke 9:62: "No procrastination. No backward looks. You can't put God's kingdom off till tomorrow. Seize the day."

It's important that we take a long hard look at where we are and invite Jesus into *that* situation. Invite Him to make the most of it. Invite Him to change you *now.* Don't wait until sometime in the future. Do it now.

> "To me, going away to college is almost like weaning you off your family. It's like halfway between being completely independent and still relying on them." — Hanna, 16

Live the life that's right in front of you; it's the life you've been given. Make the most of it.

WHAT'S THE DEAL WITH MONEY?

Money has achieved an almost godlike status in this world we live in. Look around you and you'll see person after person after person who is maybe just a little *too* interested in money.

It has become the driving goal for far too many people—their singular pursuit. Flashy cars, iPods, designer handbags, the ability to drop seven bucks into one cup at Starbucks or four bucks into a bucket of popcorn at the movies. Idolization of money is everywhere.

> "I hate money. I love to have it, but it goes away so fast. In my house, if you have money, you're expected to pay for things like gas, car insurance, that sort of thing." — Haden, 16

But money, as everything else in this world, is just a tool—a means to an end. It is a thing to be used, and to be used wisely.

Money is not the end goal of life.

Money is not the way to happiness.

Money is not worth sacrificing your life for.

Hear this well: Money is just a thing.

Now, with that in mind, money *can* be your friend, if you use it correctly.

Basically, there are three ways you can use money: You can spend it, you can save it, or you can give it away. All three of these things are inherently good, and all three of them can become bad if you take them too far.

Now, at this point in your life, you're probably happy to have a few bucks in your pocket at any given time. Honestly, that's the way most of us are, here in the real world. But, believe it or not, there are things you can do with those few bucks, patterns and habits you can set now, that will pay off later in life.

> "It's frustrating going to a private school, because
> most of the kids have money, and I don't. So for me,
> money isn't a happy thing. All my friends at school
> can afford to get the latest new thing, and, while I
> work enough to have the things I need, I can't really
> buy the things I want." — Josh, 16

Okay, this may differ depending on the denomination of the church you attend, but my personal view is that you need to give part of your paycheck, off the top, to your church.

Let's put aside the different doctrines on tithing and giving and such and just look at it in a purely practical sense: Church costs money. Your church has bills to pay, just like your parents do. They have to pay rent or some sort of building fee; there are electric bills and water bills and gas bills, depending on where you live; they have to pay for their computers and curriculum and office supplies and janitorial services and sound equipment and piano tuning and a thousand other things (and that's not even discussing the people on staff who take care of all that stuff).

So they rely on the giving of the congregation. Well, truthfully, they should rely on God, who then provides for them *through* the giving of the congregation, but you see my point.

Still, your church is not a for-profit business like any random store at the mall is. They aren't just trying to get rich by selling Jesus, if you understand what I mean. They are devoting themselves to doing the work of God full-time, and, with the support of the congregation, they are able to do that without ever giving time to a regular job, for the most part.

However, giving is important for another reason too. It's important for you personally. It shows where your heart is. It shows what you value. It gets you involved in your community of faith. And you'll feel really good to be able to help others.

I cannot stress how important charitable giving is, both to your church and to you. Sure, your church benefits by receiving money and therefore putting it to good use. But there is something about giving that cannot be backed up by statistics that causes the giver just to be happier.

Perhaps this is why Jesus said, "You're far happier giving than getting" (Acts 20:35), because He knows, unlike we do, that giving to those who need it is, in a way, one of the greatest things we can do.

DOES THAT MEAN I SHOULDN'T SPEND MONEY? ISN'T THAT WHAT A BUDGET IS — RULES ON HOW NOT TO SPEND MONEY?

What about spending? Is it bad? Not at all.

As long as you do it wisely.

See, it's easy to spend money. It's one of the easiest things in the world. Why, nowadays, you can spend money you don't even have — just get a credit card (don't really — read up on credit cards in the question and answer titled "I want a credit card. Can I have one?" on page 165).

And since it's so easy to spend money, that spending can get out of control before you realize it. This is an area where I have a bit of expertise.

Catering to my whims is something of a specialty of mine, actually. Fortunately, my whims are never too crazy — I never want an HDTV on a whim, for example. My whims are generally food- or entertainment-related; I'll want to eat at a certain

restaurant or go watch a particular movie or pick up a new book
I've been eyeing—things along those lines. Still, they are whims,
and if I listen to them, I'm in trouble. The life of a professional
writer isn't *always* a charmed one, after all.

So what should a whim-crazy chap like myself do? Wait for
it . . . yes, that's right: budget.

No, *budget* is not a bad word. If you don't like that word, we can
try a different one. How about we try on the word *plan*? Because
that's all a budget really is. It isn't a restriction on how you spend
your money; it's a way to plan out your spending so you keep it in
check, where it needs to be.

> "I set aside money for necessary stuff that I have to
> buy, and then I set aside money for spending [on stuff
> I want]. And then lately I've been setting aside extra
> money other than tithe and savings to buy a car, and so
> now I don't have much left over for spending. I have,
> like, a dollar." — Jaime, 15

Let's talk about those few bucks you have in your pocket. Do
you have anything coming up that you might need to spend it on?
Perhaps your youth group likes to hit up a standard restaurant or
coffee shop on Wednesday nights, and you're planning on throwing down a few of those bucks on the counter. Or perhaps you're
saving up for a summer missions trip or your own car, and you're
hoping to apply a few of those bucks to the unpaid balance.

You probably have some sort of something coming up that
will require money. If you have a plan (aka "budget"), you can
think ahead about that stuff and make sure you have the
bucks in your pocket when the time comes to use them.
Otherwise, you can very easily wind up spending those

bucks on Taco Bell and finding your pockets quite empty when you need the money most.

How do you make a budget? It's easy, really: Just think through whatever financial obligations you might have (Car payment? Insurance? Gas? Clothes?) and write them down. Then figure out how much money you're going to make to cover those obligations. Make sure you have enough. If you don't, figure out what you can cut out to make it, or figure out how to get more money. If you have more than you need, figure out how to use the rest of it.

Hey, this sounds suspiciously like a math problem!

WHAT ABOUT SAVING?

"My job pays more than the average job. It's not bad, but I'm saving for a missions trip, and until the very end of it, when I can see that, 'Oh, I need to give $100 here, and $200 there, and then I'll have my trip paid for,' it's like skimping, like using my spending money and my savings for my trip." — Grant, 17

Funny I should be talking about how to use your leftover money, because I was just about to transition into that third thing you can do with cash: Save it. And really, there are tons of ways you can do it, which mainly break down into two different things: You can put it in the bank or you can invest it. And this is where you'll want to seek better help than mine, because I'm pretty much at a loss as to how to do this step. I know, I know—I'm telling you to do it while not doing it myself, but that doesn't make it any less of a good idea.

I'll make you a deal: I'll start saving money along with you. Sound good?

HOW CAN SPENDING, SAVING, AND GIVING BE BAD?

I was hoping you'd ask! Well, you can understand how spending would get bad, but giving and saving? How in the world can giving and saving ever be a bad thing?

Shall we start with giving? That gets bad when you do it with the wrong heart or motivation. God doesn't want you to give out of a selfish motivation to get more, or out of guilt because someone talked you into it. Paul addresses this very issue in 2 Corinthians 9:6-7: "I want each of you to take plenty of time to think it over, and make up your own mind what you will give. That will protect you against sob stories and arm-twisting. God loves it when the giver delights in the giving."

> "**Whenever** I get money, I set aside a certain amount for offering, and the rest is more for spending. I don't really save money, which I guess I probably should, but I use the rest to buy clothes or see movies. It's hard for me to have money and not spend it."
> —Gabrielle, 16

Do you delight in giving just because God told you to do it? That's when you've found the perfect heart motivation for forking over some cash.

What about saving? How can *that* ever be bad? Again, it comes down to your heart—why are you saving? This probably won't be something you deal with right about now, but as you get older, it can become paralyzing, especially if you get into miser mode about it. When all you do is save, save, save out of fear and worry, that's bad. You've stopped relying on God to take care of you and started to rely on yourself. You've made money into a god, and that's definitely bad.

Here's how Jesus put it: "Don't hoard treasure down here where it gets eaten by moths and corroded by rust or—worse!—stolen by burglars. Stockpile treasure in heaven, where it's safe from moth and rust and burglars. It's obvious, isn't it? The place where your treasure is, is the place you will most want to be, and end up being" (Matthew 6:19-21).

There's nothing wrong with planning for the future, as long as you do it with the right heart. Which is what money all boils down to: It's a good way to know your heart. It's how to know where you want to be, and where you'll wind up.

I WANT A CREDIT CARD. CAN I HAVE ONE?

"I don't even want to mess with credit cards. I'm a horrible procrastinator, so I know I'd do the same with money." — Josh, 16

Credit card companies are *ruthless*, and it's astonishing how little they care about your well-being. When you do move on to college, you will find yourself swimming in credit card applications. Is this because they think you're awesome? They just like you a lot? They want you to feel like a real, official grown-up?

No, no, no.

The college student is the primary target of the credit card offer because the college student is, for the most part, wicked-stupid with them. Want to go out to breakfast with some friends? Throw down some plastic. Desperately need a vanilla latte, extra hot? Swipe it and it's yours. Oh, and you can't forget all those books you have to buy for your classes. And the tons of sweat-shirts and junk you'll need to advertise your university. And the gas for weekend trips home. And the . . .

Yeah. Out of all that stuff, gas for the trip home is about the only necessity. But when you have that card burning up your pocket, it's just so easy to whip it out at a moment's notice. And that's why you get hit up with all those shiny envelopes that proclaim how much you're "preapproved." They want you to use their card because they know you're likely to pay them a small fortune in interest.

Me? I got a credit card in college, telling myself I would use it only in "emergencies." Turns out my definition of emergency was often, "Well, I really want that CD" or "There's nothing to eat here, and besides, I'm in the mood for chicken-fried chicken from Chili's." I racked that sucker up so fast that when I had an *actual* emergency (some belt blew in my car that was holding the whole engine together, apparently), I had to apply for an entirely different credit card to pay for it.

Look, credit cards can be great, but you have to use them correctly. You have to make them work for you; otherwise you become a slave to them, and that's not good for you or for God. You're supposed to be a slave to only *Him*.

I'm stepping off my soapbox now.

"I don't have a credit card, and I kind of don't want one. I'm afraid to get one because if I got one, I could be, just, 'Oh, I can pay for this later,' and make bad choices." — Gabrielle, 16

I hope I haven't scared you or added to the already incredible amount of apprehension you may be feeling about college. It's a wonderful time and a wonderful experience, and I hope you get to go through it. Just be sure to go into it with your wits about you and remember that not everyone is looking out for your best interests. You'll be fine, and you'll come out of it a better — and hopefully smarter — person.

HOW CAN I USE THIS TIME TO GET READY FOR THE NEXT SIXTY OR SO YEARS OF MY LIFE?

"I think about the future, but I don't dwell on it. I don't sit in my room and think about what I'm going to be twenty years from now. I'm not sitting up there naming my children. I know people who do that, and that's a little excessive to me. There's no reason for me to want to do that." — Tyler, 17

I know, I know: You're not really asking that question. You're in your teens, and you're much more interested in getting ready for your next night at the movies, which will probably be this Friday. It is in your nature to truly and completely *not* care about being an adult, let alone one who's lived a long and productive life.

That's okay. I'm still going to talk to you about it.

Why? Because it's important, and important stuff is sometimes unwelcome. Sometimes we don't want to talk about the important stuff because it will ruin whatever good time we're having; we don't want to kill the joy in our lives with some sort of discussion about the future.

However, the future is important to talk about. I know—in other parts of this book, I told you that all you have is now and that you aren't guaranteed anything later in life and that you shouldn't worry about what lies in store for you. But you are also in a stage of life you'll never be in again, and while you shouldn't *worry* about the future, you do need to *acknowledge* it. It is there, and it will come, whether you want it to or not.

> "I think about the future a lot because I'm not entirely sure what I want to do. For the longest time I wanted to be a doctor, but that takes up a lot of your life before you ever start to get paid, and then you're in debt for a long time. I've talked to doctors and read books, and they all say it's worth it in the end, but my uncle is a doctor, and he never gets to see his family, so I think a lot about those types of things."—Michael, 17

So how can we boil down the essence of the question? There are so many facets to life, but I think a successful adult life, in the practical sense, comes down to this: Keep a healthy perspective and you'll be fine.

See, you get a wonderful opportunity in high school to practice this—this idea of keeping a healthy perspective. You may not want to hear it, and I hope I don't upset you with what I'm about to say, but I'm going to say it anyway: As a student, you are not really in the best position perspective-wise.

In general, people your age are very "really"—you don't just feel a plain emotion; you feel hyper-emotions. You aren't just "angry"; you're "really angry." Not "happy"; "really happy." "Sad," "upset," "tired," stressed"—those words aren't good enough to sum up how you feel; you need a "really" in front of 'em.

I'm sure *you're* the exception to the stereotype, but just keep reading so you can pass this information on to your friends.

The thing is, life in general is so much better if you can grab hold of those emotions and pull them out of the "really" stage and into the place they're supposed to be. Reserve the "really" stuff for God. Righteous anger, God-given peace, unspeakable joy—those are the times to break out the "really." All the standard emotions you have that make you human? Just treat them without all the drama and you'll be fine.

Because the drama won't get you anywhere. I'll give you an example.

I have a car with a very troublesome driver's-side window. This thing is so annoying. It's fine when I roll it down, but when I go to roll it back up, it tilts forward and gets stuck. I have to guide it up with one hand while rolling it up with the other, and it gets on my nerves, especially if I'm on the highway or some other place where rushing wind in my face is unwelcome.

I got it fixed the other day, which lasted for about three days. They were three awesome days, but they were short-lived because that stupid window started messing up again. And boy, did I get mad about it. I couldn't believe that the repair place had just charged me sixty-five bucks to fix the window and it wasn't even fixed. Argh!

So I was all mad about that. Then, later that night, my wife and I went out to dinner and the restaurant messed up our appetizer—twice! Argh!

The next day, I got into an argument with my wife over something so trivial and small I forget what it was about. It was Sunday, so I tromped off to church all grumpy about my recent run of bad luck.

And then my pastor started talking about these three German missionaries in Turkey. Maybe you've heard about them. They were working to spread the gospel in that predominantly Muslim nation when some of their supposed converts turned out to be extremists who tortured and murdered them for their faith in Christ.

Crummy window? Burned appetizer? Stupid argument? Yeah. Those all seemed pretty dumb. Finally.

I was able to see them for what they were. That story about the German missionaries in Turkey had given me perspective. I had been so immersed in my own minor problems that I'd completely forgotten about the larger ones of the world. I'd focused on the wrong thing.

I'd lost my perspective.

"From the time I was two years old until I was about fourteen, I had my mind set: I was going to go to Juilliard and I was going to become a ballerina. There were no ifs, ands, or buts about it—that's what I was going to do. And then I broke my ankle, and they told me I couldn't do as intense stuff anymore. It was never going to happen. Life happens and you have to go on. You can't always make all these decisions at one point in time because you don't know what's going to happen."—Kaitlin, 17

In the long run, those things we make a big deal out of are a smaller deal than we could ever really imagine. It goes back to a sentence found in James 4:14: Our lives are "nothing but a wisp of fog, catching a brief bit of sun before disappearing."

Now, don't get all "really" on me with that passage and say, "Well, Adam, that means life is pointless. Why should I even try? What's keeping me from just having fun, or sitting on the edge of my bed all depressed?"

Life isn't pointless; it's just *short*—which makes it have even *more* of a point. If you had, say, a zillion years to live, then it might be okay to waste a decade or two playing Xbox 360 or whatever new game system comes out next week. But since life is so short, you have all the more reason to live it with God's perspective instead of your own.

Don't believe me? Check out what the Bible has to say about it: "If you're serious about living this new resurrection life with Christ, act like it. Pursue the things over which Christ presides. Don't shuffle along, eyes to the ground, absorbed with the things right in front of you. Look up, and be alert to what is going on around Christ—that's where the action is. See things from his perspective" (Colossians 3:1-2).

See what I mean? I'd become absorbed with the things right in front of me: my window, the food, the fight. I'd lost the action.

Learn to walk with your head up, aware of Christ's perspective on the world. Everything else will take care of itself.

WHY SHOULD I CARE ABOUT THE FUTURE?

Whether you acknowledge it or not, the future is ahead of you. And not just your immediate future, like prom or summer vacation. I mean stuff like college, and then a job, and family, and mid-life crisis, and having teenagers of your own, and retirement, and living out your golden years working crossword puzzles all day and eating dinner at 4:30 in the afternoon.

It's there.

Waiting.

There's nothing you can do to stop it, so you might as well embrace it.

> "I think that God has a plan for everybody, so I'm going to take it as He gives it to me." — Jenava, 17

Live in the now; take advantage of the moment life has given you, because you never know when it'll be over. But at the same time, plan for a long life. Plan for the future.

> "When I was in sixth grade, my teachers would show videos telling us to start planning for college now, to check into this or look into that. It freaked me out. I was little and thinking, *I have to start planning; I have to start doing all these things. I have to get Distinguished Graduate or win the Distinguished Service Award.* Now I realize that life doesn't always go as you plan it."
> — Jennifer, 17

You aren't invincible. Hopefully you know that by now. You may feel like it, but you aren't. So take care of yourself.

Take care of yourself so that you can be a good student.

Take care of yourself so that, when the time comes, you can be a good spouse. You know, your spouse will have rights to your body that you won't—think of that before you sleep around or mess around with drugs or anything else that screws up your body.

Take care of yourself so that you can be a good parent. Someone once told me, when I was about thirteen years old, that the way I treated my parents was the way my kids were going to treat me. That scared the pooey out of me, so I respected my parents like nobody's business. And you know what? So far, it's been true.

Take care of yourself so that you can be a good steward of God's resources. He wants to give you tons—show Him now that He can trust you with it.

"I'm a senior and I still don't know what I want to do. I know people who have graduated and still don't know what they want to do. I know people in their forties who still don't know what they want to do. You have to take life as it comes. You should prepare for stuff, yes, but you can't plan everything out."—Jenava, 17

Take care of yourself so that you can be a servant. God has huge plans for you, and they've already started. The more you submit to His will now, the farther down the road you'll go—and you'll be amazed where you find yourself.

Take care of yourself so that you can have a proper perspective on life. Take care of yourself so that, above all things, you can trust your heavenly Father. That's where it begins and ends, this life, and that's my ultimate prayer for you. That you will trust Him like crazy, no matter what life throws at you. Because He's good, like no other.

AUTHOR

Adam Palmer is a former high school student who made it through all four years alive and relatively unscathed. After that, he spent some time in college, then eventually wound up writing books for a living, some of which are *Taming a Liger: Unexpected Spiritual Lessons from Napoleon Dynamite* and the novels *Mooch* and *Knuckle Sandwich*. He lives in Tulsa, Oklahoma, with his family and his golden retriever, who recently graduated from obedience school.

Check out these other great titles from NavPress!